THE RIGHT TO DUE PROCESS

THE RIGHT TO DUE PROCESS

Other books in this series:

The Bill of Rights

THE RIGHT TO DUE PROCESS

Edited by Kimberly Troisi-Paton

Bruce Glassman, *Vice President*
Bonnie Szumski, *Publisher*
Helen Cothran, *Managing Editor*
Scott Barbour, *Series Editor*

GREENHAVEN PRESS
An imprint of Thomson Gale, a part of The Thomson Corporation

THOMSON

GALE

Detroit • New York • San Francisco • San Diego • New Haven, Conn.
Waterville, Maine • London • Munich

THOMSON

GALE

Cover credit: © Shelley Gazin/The Image Works. In Los Angeles, California, an attorney meets with her client, a juvenile offender in jail.

LIBRARY OF CONGRESS CATALOGING-IN-PUBLICATION DATA

The right to due process / Kimberly Troisi-Paton, book editor.
    p. cm. — (Bill of rights)
Includes bibliographical references and index.
ISBN 0-7377-1941-9 (lib. : alk. paper)
    1. Due process of law—United States—History. I. Troisi-Paton, Kimberly.
II. Bill of Rights (San Diego, Calif.)

KF4765.R544 2005
347.73'5—dc22

2005040253

The Bill of Rights   CONTENTS

Chapter 1: The History of the Right to Due Process

Chapter 2: Due Process and the Rights of Accused Criminals

The Court ruled that, based on an inferred right to privacy, a woman has the right to an abortion.

Appendix

"I cannot agree with those who think of the Bill of Rights as an 18th century straightjacket, unsuited for this age. . . . The evils it guards against are not only old, they are with us now, they exist today."
—Hugo Black, associate justice of the
U.S. Supreme Court, 1937–1971

The Bill of Rights codifies the freedoms most essential to American democracy. Freedom of speech, freedom of religion, the right to bear arms, the right to a trial by a jury of one's peers, the right to be free from cruel and unusual punishment—these are just a few of the liberties that the Founding Fathers thought it necessary to spell out in the first ten amendments to the U.S. Constitution.

While the document itself is quite short (consisting of fewer than five hundred words), and while the liberties it protects often seem straightforward, the Bill of Rights has been a source of debate ever since its creation. Throughout American history, the rights the document protects have been tested and reinterpreted. Again and again, individuals perceiving violations of their rights have sought redress in the courts. The courts in turn have struggled to decipher the original intent of the founders as well as the need to accommodate changing societal norms and values.

The ultimate responsibility for addressing these claims has fallen to the U.S. Supreme Court. As the highest court in the nation, it is the Supreme Court's role to interpret the Constitution. The Court has considered numerous cases in which people have accused government of impinging on their rights. In the process, the Court has established a body of case law and precedents that have, in a sense, defined the Bill of Rights. In doing so, the Court has often reversed itself and introduced new ideas and approaches that have altered the legal meaning of the rights contained in the Bill of Rights. As a general rule, the Court has erred on the side of caution, upholding and expanding the rights of individuals rather than restricting them.

An example of this trend is the definition of cruel and unusual punishment. The Eighth Amendment specifically states, "Excessive bail shall not be required, nor excessive fines imposed, nor cruel and unusual punishments inflicted." However, over the years the Court has had to grapple with defining what constitutes "cruel and unusual punishment." In colonial America, punishments for crimes included branding, the lopping off of ears, and whipping. Indeed, these punishments were considered lawful at the time the Bill of Rights was written. Obviously, none of these punishments are legal today. In order to justify outlawing certain types of punishment that are deemed repugnant by the majority of citizens, the Court has ruled that it must consider the prevailing opinion of the masses when making such decisions. In overturning the punishment of a man stripped of his citizenship, the Court stated in 1958 that it must rely on society's "evolving standards of decency" when determining what constitutes cruel and unusual punishment. Thus the definition of cruel and unusual is not frozen to include only the types of punishment that were illegal at the time of the framing of the Bill of Rights; specific modes of punishment can be rejected as society deems them unjust.

Another way that the Courts have interpreted the Bill of Rights to expand individual liberties is through the process of "incorporation." Prior to the passage of the Fourteenth Amendment, the Bill of Rights was thought to prevent only the federal government from infringing on the rights listed in the document. However, the Fourteenth Amendment, which was passed in the wake of the Civil War, includes the words, ". . . nor shall any state deprive any person of life, liberty, or property, without due process of law; nor deny to any person within its jurisdiction the equal protection of the laws." Citing this passage, the Court has ruled that many of the liberties contained in the Bill of Rights apply to state and local governments as well as the federal government. This process of incorporation laid the legal foundation for the civil rights movement—most specifically the 1954 *Brown v. Board of Education* ruling that put an end to legalized segregation.

As these examples reveal, the Bill of Rights is not static. It truly is a living document that is constantly being reinterpreted and redefined. The Bill of Rights series captures this vital aspect of one of America's most cherished founding texts. Each volume in the series focuses on one particular right protected in the Bill of Rights. Through the use of primary and secondary sources, the right's evolution is traced from colonial times to the present. Primary sources include landmark Supreme Court rulings, speeches by prominent experts, and editorials. Secondary sources include historical analyses, law journal articles, book excerpts, and magazine articles. Each book also includes several features to facilitate research, including a bibliography, an annotated table of contents, an annotated list of relevant Supreme Court cases, an introduction, and an index. These elements help to make the Bill of Rights series a fascinating and useful tool for examining the fundamental liberties of American democracy.

No person shall be deprived "of life, liberty, or property, without due process of law." This is a concept so critical to the notion of democracy in the United States that it appears twice in the amendments to the Constitution: first, in the Fifth Amendment, ratified with the initial Bill of Rights in 1791; then, in the Fourteenth Amendment, ratified after the Civil War in 1868. Yet in neither of those places are the various components of the phrase clearly defined. For better or worse, this lack of clarity has left the interpretation of "due process" subject to the prevailing societal norms of any given moment in history. As a result, as stated by former Supreme Court justice Benjamin N. Cardozo, the constitutional guarantee of due process truly "varies from age to age."[1]

Procedural Due Process

Early attempts to define due process focused on the latter part of the guarantee—no deprivation of rights should occur "without due process of law." The Supreme Court examined the procedures that were used as a means to any given legal end, such as the legal procedures used to collect debts or to punish criminals. The Court performed an analysis of the procedures at issue and created a body of law now known as "procedural due process" cases. With the first procedural due process cases, great frustration arose from the fact that, in the words of former Supreme Court justice Benjamin R. Curtis, the "constitution contains no description of those processes which it was intended to allow or forbid. It does not even declare what principles are to be applied to ascertain whether it be due process."[2]

At first the Court determined that a procedure generally constituted due process if the procedure did not violate the Constitution and was similar to procedures used in England. Later, the Court simplified this analysis by dropping the comparison to English law. In *Hurtado v. California* (1884), due process was defined as "any legal proceeding enforced by public authority . . . in furtherance of the general public good, which regards and preserves . . . principles of liberty and justice."[3] In the 1937 case *Palko v. Connecticut*, the Court further modified this test by asking whether the legal proceeding in question was "implicit in the concept of ordered liberty" such that it involved one of the "fundamental principles of liberty and justice which lie at the base of all our civil and political institutions."[4] In other words, the Court ruled that a procedure would only be considered a violation of due process if it impinged on a right that the Court deemed "fundamental."

Over time, the Court essentially has created a checklist of procedural elements that make up proper process. The list includes such protections as appropriate notice of an impending legal action, proper opportunity for all parties to have their sides of the case heard, an opportunity to be represented by counsel, and a hearing before a neutral judge or other decision maker. However, this focus on a procedural analysis created results that probably would not be acceptable under today's due process standards. For example, in 1927 the Court examined a Virginia law that permitted the sterilization of institutionalized mental health patients in a case called *Buck v. Bell*. Justice Oliver Wendell Holmes, one of the most esteemed jurists of all time, found that a court order calling for the sterilization of an institutionalized eighteen-year-old woman was proper. The Court determined that adequate legal procedures were in place, including a hearing on notice. Noting the woman's family history of mental illness, Holmes infamously commented, "Three generations of imbeciles are enough."[5] Under the standards applied at the time, the institutionalized woman had received due process.

Substantive Due Process

Later cases departed from this procedural analysis and focused on the first part of the due process guarantee—protection against deprivation of "life, liberty, or property." The Court began to focus on the end result of a legal proceeding (the substance of the case) and not just the means to it (the procedure). The attempt to define the various substantive rights at stake is now known as "substantive due process."

Substantive due process analysis brought with it problems similar to the early procedural due process cases. The particular rights at issue were not mentioned anywhere in the Constitution. Rather, they were grounded in the concepts protected by due process—life, liberty, and property. However, the concepts of liberty and property also were not clearly explained in the text of the Constitution. As Cardozo states:

> Liberty is not defined. Its limits are not mapped and charted. How shall they be known? Does liberty mean the same thing for successive generations? May restraints that were arbitrary yesterday be useful and rational and therefore lawful today? May restraints that are arbitrary today become useful and rational and therefore lawful tomorrow? I have no doubt that the answer to these [last two] questions must be yes.[6]

Cardozo's questions strike at the heart of the due process quandary—due process and its substantive and procedural components mean different things to different people. And history has proven his answer correct.

Today, substantive due process analysis is both criticized and lauded as "creating" new rights. For instance, recent substantive due process cases have focused on individual autonomy, or privacy, as an important liberty interest. Privacy is a liberty not delineated anywhere in the Constitution. Yet the privacy interest today includes rights that were not even acknowledged by the Court only decades ago: the right of all individuals to use contraception, of women to obtain an abortion, of competent patients to refuse life-sustaining medical treatment, and of same-sex couples to engage in sexual relationships. Many Americans cannot envision a world without these rights, while many others wish these rights still did not exist.

The Evolution of Liberty and Due Process

At times the evolution of liberty interests in the face of varying public viewpoints has required the Court to overrule its own precedent. For example, in the 1986 case *Bowers v. Hardwick* the Court determined that the due process clauses do not create a privacy right for homosexuals in consensual relationships. In 2003 the Court considered the same issue and specifically overruled *Bowers*, granting a privacy right to same-sex couples. Calling to mind Judge Cardozo's comments on liberty, the Court stated in *Lawrence v. Texas:*

> Had those who drew and ratified the Due Process Clauses of the Fifth Amendment or the Fourteenth Amendment known the components of liberty in its manifold possibilities, they might have been more specific. They did not presume to have this insight. They knew times can blind us to certain truths and later generations can see that laws once thought necessary and proper in fact serve only to oppress. As the Constitution endures, persons in every generation can invoke its principles in their own search for greater freedom.[7]

Given the consistent expansion of the privacy interest in the past few decades, it is not surprising that the Court overruled its prior *Bowers* decision. Indeed, it is likely that if today's Court examined a case such as *Buck v. Bell*, the original result would no longer be acceptable on substantive due process grounds, no matter what the procedural provisions in place.

Yet, despite the recent emphasis on substantive due process, procedural due process is still an indispensable component of the Constitution's guarantees. The Court experienced a renewed focus on procedure in the summer of 2004 when it heard several cases involving individuals detained at the U.S. Naval Station at Guantánamo Bay, Cuba. The individuals, labeled "enemy combatants" by the U.S. government, were being held but not necessarily charged with a specific crime in the aftermath of the events of September 11, 2001, and the wars in Afghanistan and Iraq. The complainants argued that they should not be detained without access to an attorney or a trial. The government responded that adequate process had been provided to the detainees, considering the national security issues at stake and the government's right to restrict wartime access to the court system.

In what is possibly the most significant of these cases, *Hamdi v. Rumsfeld*, the Supreme Court reached a plurality decision, which means that no single opinion of the Court carried a majority of the nine justices. The fractured *Hamdi* Court demonstrated that due process can vary not only from age to age, but also from justice to justice. The plurality opinion, which permitted an "enemy combatant" detainee the chance to contest the detention before a neutral decision maker, emphasized the importance of upholding individual rights even in times of national crisis: "It is during our most challenging and uncertain moments that our Nation's commitment to due process is most severely tested; and it is in those times that we must preserve our commitment at home to the principles for which we fight abroad."[8]

The Right Balance

The due process cases from 2004 demonstrate why the law must be embodied both with principles that remain unchanged throughout history as well as flexible, fluid concepts that cannot have static and ironclad definitions. The framers of the Constitution could not have envisioned the catastrophic events of September 11, yet the fundamental principles for which they struggled to find words have given Americans the tools to cope with the results of that day.

While disagreement about due process may fuel debate about procedure and substance in perpetuity, this disagreement is constructive. The challenge is to strike the right balance between holding fast to the framers' perceived original intent and applying that intent to new, unique circumstances. The Court's task is to honor the principles embodied in a document that has been successful in preserving freedom for over two hundred years, while modifying the component parts to meet the expectations of each subsequent generation.

Notes

1. Benjamin N. Cardozo, *The Nature of the Judicial Process: The Storrs Lectures Delivered at Yale University.* New Haven, CT: Yale University Press, 1921, p. 83.

2. Benjamin R. Curtis, *Murray's Lessee v. Hoboken Land & Improvement Co.,* 1855.

3. Stanley Matthews, *Hurtado v. California,* 1884.

4. Benjamin N. Cardozo, *Palko v. Connecticut,* 1937.

5. Oliver Wendell Holmes, *Buck v. Bell,* 1927.

6. Cardozo, *The Nature of the Judicial Process,* pp. 76–77.

7. Anthony Kennedy, *Lawrence v. Texas,* 2003.

8. Sandra Day O'Connor, *Hamdi v. Rumsfeld,* 2004.

CHAPTER ONE

The History of the Right to Due Process

The Bill of Rights

The Origins and Evolution of Due Process

John V. Orth

John V. Orth is a professor of law at the University of North Carolina, Chapel Hill. He has authored several books and articles about judicial power in the United States. His publications have been cited by many courts, including the U.S. Supreme Court.

The following selection is excerpted from the introductory chapter of Orth's book *Due Process of Law: A Brief History*. Orth summarizes the history behind the Constitution's due process clauses and touches on the major issues that have arisen since the U.S. Supreme Court began to apply the clauses. Orth demonstrates how, from the seemingly simple phrase "due process of law," two doctrines of due process have evolved. These two doctrines are known as procedural due process and substantive due process. The doctrine of procedural due process holds that fair procedures must be followed in both criminal and civil cases in order to ensure the rights of individuals. The doctrine of substantive due process holds that there are fundamental rights that are not explicitly stated in the Constitution.

One of the most frequently asked questions in American constitutional history has been, what is required by the constitutional guarantee of "due process of law"? The phrase appears twice in the U.S. Constitution—in the Fifth Amendment in the Bill of Rights, which prohibits the federal government from depriving any person of "life, liberty, or property, without due process of law," and in the Fourteenth Amendment, adopted almost one hundred years later in the aftermath of the Civil War, which extends the same prohibition to the states: "No State shall . . . deprive any person of life, liberty, or property, without due process of law." What exactly does due process require? . . .

Can a law make a man a judge in his own case? Can a law take the property of A and give it to B? These questions more than any others were used over the centuries to illuminate the demands of due process. They are not questions asked only in American law; they can arise in any legal system. And "due process of law" was not a phrase invented by American constitution-writers: it was picked up by them from the rich tradition of English constitutionalism in which they were formed. From this perspective, the War of American Independence can be regarded as a civil war within the British Empire over the meaning and future course of the British constitution. Unlike their French counterparts a few years later, American Revolutionaries did not lay claim to "the rights of man" but to "the rights of Englishmen."

The Law of the Land

English rights were first memorably expressed in Magna Carta in 1215. Among many other things, the notorious King John was forced by his rebellious barons to promise that "nullus liber homo capiatur, vel imprisonetur, aut disseisiatur, aut utlagetur, aut exulatur, aut aliquo modo destruatur, nec super eum ibimus, nec super eum mittemus, nisi per legale judicium parium suorum vel per legem terrae" (no free man shall be taken or imprisoned or disseised or outlawed or exiled, or in any way ruined, nor will we go or send against him, except by the lawful judgment of his peers or by the law of the land). What exactly that meant in the Middle Ages is not completely clear, and scholars continue to debate the point. Over the ensuing centuries, Magna Carta was even lost sight of temporarily, but in the constitutional controversies of the seventeenth century, as other English monarchs encroached on English liberties, it was rediscovered and gained renewed prominence.

Sir Edward Coke, a contemporary of . . . [English author William] Shakespeare, wrote influential commentaries on

English statutes, restating and in the process enlarging the demands of Magna Carta: the "law of the land," Coke said, meant the common law, and the common law required "due process." The earliest American state constitutions clung to the words of the Great Charter and safeguarded the "law of the land"; a few of them still do. But the drafters of the federal Bill of Rights opted for Coke's phrase, and "due process of law" has been standard American usage ever since. Most state constitutions today follow the federal example, and those that continue to guarantee the "law of the land" are routinely interpreted to require the same thing.

In its English origin the guarantee of due process (or the law of the land) was a restraint on the sovereign: before King John or his royal officers could take action against a person, certain procedures had to be followed, procedures designed to ensure fairness. Fair procedures are still at the heart of due process today; in modern parlance they are often expressed by the somewhat different phrase, "the rule of law." Although a number of elements constitute the rule of law, the procedural essentials can be encapsulated in the requirement of an accessible, impartial, and effective decision maker or, to put it simply, a good judge. Can a law make a man a judge in his own case? The question can be used to test the procedural fairness of any legal system by highlighting one of its most essential features, whether cases are decided by an independent decision maker, one with no personal stake in the outcome and no fear of retribution from the powers that be if the case is decided one way or the other. It can be used to test, in other words, whether the system guarantees the rule of law; in the common law system it signifies respect for the traditional procedures of the "law of the land" or "due process of law."

The Substantive Part of Due Process

Six hundred and fifty years after Magna Carta, in the last quarter of the nineteenth century, due process in America had come to include significant constitutional limitations on legislative power as well. No longer exclusively concerned with how the executive proceeded, due process had developed a concern with what the legislature did; that is, due process had acquired a substantive dimension. The U.S. Supreme Court justice Samuel Miller had the historical perspective to recognize the contrast. In 1878 in *Davidson v. New Orleans* he wrote on behalf of the Court: "It is easy to see that when the great barons of England wrung from King John, at the point of the sword, the concession that neither their lives nor their property should be disposed of by the crown, except as provided by the law of the land, they meant by 'law of the land' the ancient and customary [procedural] laws of the English people, or laws enacted by the [local] Parliament of which those barons were a controlling element. It was not in their minds, therefore to protect themselves against the enactment of [substantive] laws by the [national] Parliament of England." But, he continued, the Fourteenth Amendment directed the Supreme Court's attention to action by the states. "Can a State make anything due process of law which, by its own legislation, it chooses to declare such?" he asked rhetorically, and promptly answered on behalf of his brethren: "To affirm this is to hold that the prohibition to the States is of no avail, or has no application where the invasion of private rights is effected under the forms of State legislation. It seems to us that a statute which declares in terms, and without more, that the full and exclusive title of a described piece of land, which is now in A, shall be and is hereby vested in B, would, if effectual, deprive A of his property without due process of law, within the meaning of the constitutional provision." Taking from A and giving to B had become, in other words, the shorthand to describe what substantive due process was designed to prevent. As one modern scholar [John Harrison] put it, quoting *Davidson*, the A-to-B paradigm was "every nineteenth century lawyer's favorite example of an unconstitutional statute—albeit one that was unconstitutional for various different reasons."

Making a man a judge in his own case was a bad thing, all could agree. So was taking from A and giving to B, but what the problem was exactly was not so clear. A great many cases, some of them quite different, could be comprehended within the seemingly simple A-to-B paradigm, and that ambiguity allowed a good deal of out-of-sight judicial development. At first, the taking was assumed to involve A's property: the classic formula was, in fact, as Justice Miller put it, a law that took A's *land* and gave it to B. Law has always been about power, and in medieval England, at the origin of the common law, power was intimately tied up with land ownership, so the early common law showed a precocious interest in property. For centuries, land law remained at the center of things, elaborated into an increasingly complex system with its own vocabulary and concepts, some of them quite fantastic. But property was never confined to land, and as concepts of property expanded over time to include a host of intangible interests, so did the scope of due process.

The Changing Nature of Substantive Rights

Beginning in the eighteenth century, in the years before the American Revolution, the common law was forced to confront new economic arrangements with momentous consequences for the distribution of power within society. International trade, spurred by Britain's world-girdling empire, required the organization of production and the transportation of goods over vast distances. Frontier conditions in America put unheard of amounts of land on the market, much of it purchased on installment contracts or with complicated loan agreements. In the mobilization of the new productive forces, contract assumed an importance that was to rival, if not surpass, property; wealth and power now lay in agreements as much as in ownership. As the emphasis of the common law shifted from property to contract, so the cases involving due process shifted as well. If the law was to protect contract as zealously as it protected property, a new view of due process was required. Liberty, it was recalled, was covered as well as property, and concern about taking away A's property was soon rivaled by concern about taking away A's liberty, specifically A's liberty to enter into enforceable agreements or, as it was more commonly called, A's freedom of contract.

The shift from property to contract by no means marked the end of the story. In time, as experience with takings accumulated, it appeared that what was taken and who got it

were less important than that any kind of taking had occurred. The new focus on individual agreement had redi-
rected attention away from things and toward persons.
Liberated from a preoccupation with property, the law increasingly recognized less tangible interests, at first in labor
but later in private matters such as reproductive rights. In
the twentieth century, as the emphasis in the law shifted
from contract to civil rights, so the cases shifted from concern with interfering with A's freedom of contract to concern
with interfering with A's freedom in other regards.

Beginning as the history of proper procedure, the history
of due process became the history of substantive guarantees
as well. Procedure is a perennial concern of the courts, but
substance varies with the times, as economic and social demands come and go.

A Colonial Law Guaranteeing Due Process

General Assembly of Maryland

As colonial Americans struggled to establish their autonomy from the British Crown, Virginia took the lead in creating a system of self-government with an elected legislature in 1606. Massachusetts followed in 1629, then Maryland in 1632. The charters that established these governing systems were basic statements that the colonists were entitled to the same rights as their English counterparts across the Atlantic.

With their legislatures in place, the colonists were then able to clarify exactly what their rights were. In 1639 the General Assembly of Maryland passed a law entitled An Act for the Liberties of the People. The act specifically provided for due process; no colonist would lose liberty or property unless the loss occurred according to the laws of the province of Maryland. It was a simple law that created a significant guarantee. Some commentators have even called the act the first American Bill of Rights.

Be it Enacted By the Lord Proprietarie of this Province of and with the advice and approbation of the freemen of the same that all the Inhabitants of this Province being Christians (Slaves excepted) Shall have and enjoy all such rights liberties immunities priviledges and free customs within this Province as any naturall born subject of England hath or ought to have or enjoy in the Realm of England by force or vertue of the common law or Statute Law of England (saveing in such Cases as the same are or may be altered or changed by the Laws and ordinances of this Province)

General Assembly of Maryland, *An Act for the Liberties of the People,* 1639.

And Shall not be imprisoned nor disseissed or dispossessed of their freehold goods or Chattels or be out Lawed Exiled or otherwise destroyed fore judged or punished then according to the Laws of this province saveing to the Lord proprietarie and his heirs all his rights and prerogatives by reason of his domination and Seigniory over this Province and the people of the same This Act to Continue till the end of the next Generall Assembly

CHAPTER TWO

Due Process and the Rights of Accused Criminals

The Bill of Rights

Protection Against Double Jeopardy Is Not a Fundamental Right

Benjamin N. Cardozo

The following selection was excerpted from the 1937 Supreme Court opinion in *Palko v. Connecticut.* At Frank Palko's trial for first-degree murder, the jury had returned a verdict of guilty on a count of second-degree murder. The difference in a degree was huge—it meant life in prison instead of a death sentence for Palko. The prosecutor for the state of Connecticut appealed the verdict, citing several errors of law that he believed had occurred at the trial. A Connecticut state law allowed the prosecution to make such an appeal. One of the alleged errors involved the judge's instructions to the jury about the difference between first- and second-degree murder.

Palko was retried. At the second trial he objected that the new trial placed him in "double jeopardy," in violation of the Fifth Amendment, which forbids trying a suspect twice for the same crime. However, the Fifth Amendment places limits on the federal government, and Palko was being tried by a state government. Accordingly, Palko hinged his double jeopardy argument on the due process clause of the Fourteenth Amendment. The language of that amendment provides, "nor shall any State deprive any person of life, liberty, or property without due process of law." Palko argued that this language meant that if the federal government cannot place someone in double jeopardy, then a state government cannot either.

Unfortunately for Palko, no courts agreed with him. The trial court overruled his objection, and the second trial proceeded. Palko was convicted of first-degree murder and ap-

Benjamin N. Cardozo, opinion, *Palko v. Connecticut,* 302 U.S. 319, December 6, 1937.

pealed all the way to the U.S. Supreme Court. The Court refused to overturn his conviction in 1937, and Palko was executed in 1938.

Justice Benjamin N. Cardozo wrote the opinion in *Palko v. Connecticut*. Having previously served as the chief judge on the New York Court of Appeals and written volumes on the nature of the judicial process, Justice Cardozo was one of the most scholarly, influential, and respected judges of the twentieth century.

In *Palko*, Cardozo sorted through the case law to date in an effort to resolve the question of "incorporation." At issue was whether, in light of the Fourteenth Amendment, the Bill of Rights protects citizens from state government actions in the same way that it protects them from federal government actions. Cardozo's answer was that only those rights in the Bill of Rights that involve certain fundamental principles that are essential to the preservation of ordered liberty are to be applied by incorporation against the states. At the time, freedom from double jeopardy was not considered a fundamental right as compared to other rights, such as the First Amendment's speech-related freedoms. Furthermore, Cardozo reasoned that the state's right to have a trial free from legal error is just as important as a defendant's right to an error-free trial.

Cardozo's attempt to define which rights were fundamental remains one of the clearest articulations of a very complex doctrine. However, over the next several decades his seemingly firm distinctions blurred as the law of criminal procedure evolved one case at a time.

The argument for appellant is that whatever is forbidden by the Fifth Amendment is forbidden by the Fourteenth also. The Fifth Amendment, which is not directed to the States, but solely to the federal government, creates immunity from double jeopardy. No person shall be 'subject for the same offense to be twice put in jeopardy of life or limb.' The Fourteenth Amendment ordains, 'nor shall any State deprive any person of life, liberty, or property, without due process of law.' To retry a defendant, . . . subjects him, it is said, to double jeopardy in violation of the Fifth Amendment, if the prosecution is one on behalf of the United States. From this the consequence is said to follow that there is a denial of life or liberty without due process of law, if the prosecution is one on behalf of the people of a state. . . .

We do not find it profitable to mark the precise limits of the prohibition of double jeopardy in federal prosecutions. The subject was much considered in *Kepner v. United States*, decided in 1904 by a closely divided court. The view was there expressed for a majority of the court that the prohibition was not confined to jeopardy in a new and independent case. It forbade jeopardy in the same case if the new trial was at the instance of the government and not upon defendant's motion. All this may be assumed for the purpose of the case at hand, though the dissenting opinions show how much was to be said in favor of a different ruling. Right-minded men, as we learn from those opinions, could reasonably, even if mistakenly, believe that a second trial was lawful in prosecutions subject to the Fifth Amendment, if it was all in the same case. Even more plainly, right-minded men could reasonably believe that in espousing that conclusion they were not favoring a practice repugnant to the conscience of mankind. Is double jeopardy in such circumstances, if double jeopardy it must be called, a denial of due process forbidden to the States? . . .

Only Fundamental Rights Are Protected from State Infringement

We have said that in appellant's view the Fourteenth Amendment is to be taken as embodying the prohibitions of the Fifth. His thesis is even broader. Whatever would be a violation of the original bill of rights (Amendments 1 to 8) if done by the federal government is now equally unlawful by force of the Fourteenth Amendment if done by a state. There is no such general rule.

The Fifth Amendment provides, among other things, that no person shall be held to answer for a capital or otherwise infamous crime unless on presentment or indictment of a grand jury. This court has held that, in prosecutions by a state, presentment or indictment by a grand jury may give way to [be replaced by] informations at the instance of a public officer. The Fifth Amendment provides also that no person shall be compelled in any criminal case to be a witness against himself. This court has said that, in prosecutions by a state, the exemption will fail if the state elects to end it. The Sixth Amendment calls for a jury trial in criminal cases and the Seventh for a jury trial in civil cases at common law where the value in controversy shall exceed $20. This court has ruled that consistently with those amendments trial by jury may be modified by a state or abolished altogether.

On the other hand, the due process clause of the Fourteenth Amendment may make it unlawful for a state to abridge by its statutes the freedom of speech which the First Amendment safeguards against encroachment by the Congress or the like freedom of the press, or the free exercise of religion, or the right of peaceable assembly, without which speech would be unduly trammeled, or the right of one accused of crime to the benefit of counsel. In these and other situations immunities that are valid as against the federal government by force of the specific pledges of particular amendments have been found to be implicit in the concept of ordered liberty, and thus, through the Fourteenth Amendment, become valid as against the states.

The line of division may seem to be wavering and broken if there is a hasty catalogue of the cases on the one side and the other. Reflection and analysis will induce a different view. There emerges the perception of a rationalizing principle which gives to discrete instances a proper order and coherence. The right to trial by jury and the immunity from prosecution except as the result of an indictment may have value and importance. Even so, they are not of the very essence of a scheme of ordered liberty. To abolish them is not to violate [as stated in *Synder v. Massachusetts* (1934)] a 'principle of justice so rooted in the traditions and conscience of our people as to be ranked as fundamental.' Few would be so narrow or provincial as to maintain that a fair and enlightened system of justice would be impossible without them. What is true of jury trials and indictments is true also, as the cases show, of the immunity from compulsory self-incrimination. This too might be lost, and justice still be done. Indeed, today as in the past there are students of our penal system who look upon the immunity as a mischief rather than a benefit, and who would limit its scope, or destroy it altogether. No doubt there would remain the need to give protection against torture, physical or mental. Justice, however, would not perish if the accused were subject to a duty to respond to orderly inquiry. The exclusion of these immunities and privileges from the privileges and immunities protected against the action of the States has not been arbitrary or casual. It has been dictated by a study and appreciation of the meaning, the essential implications, of liberty itself.

Due Process and Fundamental Rights

We reach a different plane of social and moral values when we pass to the privileges and immunities that have been taken over from the earlier articles of the Federal Bill of Rights and brought within the Fourteenth Amendment by a process of absorption. These in their origin were effective against the federal government alone. If the Fourteenth Amendment has absorbed them, the process of absorption has had its source in the belief that neither liberty nor justice would exist if they were sacrificed. This is true, for illustration, of freedom of thought and speech. Of that freedom one may say that it is the matrix, the indispensable condition, of nearly every other form of freedom. With rare aberrations a pervasive recognition of that truth can be traced in our history, political and legal. So it has come about that the domain of liberty, withdrawn by the Fourteenth Amendment from encroachment by the states, has been enlarged by latter-day judgments to include liberty of the mind as well as liberty of action. . . . Fundamental too in the concept of due process, and so in that of liberty, is the thought that condemnation shall be rendered only after trial. The hearing, moreover, must be a real one, not a sham or a pretense. For that reason, ignorant defendants in a capital case were held to have been condemned unlawfully when in truth, though not in form, they were refused the aid of counsel. The decision did not turn upon the fact that the benefit of counsel would have been guaranteed to the defendants by the provisions of the Sixth Amendment if they had been prosecuted in a federal court. The decision turned upon the fact that in the particular situation laid before us in the evidence the benefit of counsel was essential to the substance of a hearing.

Our survey of the cases serves, we think, to justify the statement that the dividing line between them, if not unfaltering throughout its course, has been true for the most part to a unifying principle. On which side of the line the case made out by the appellant has appropriate location must be the next inquiry and the final one. Is that kind of double jeopardy to which the statute has subjected him a hardship so acute and shocking that our policy will not endure it? Does it violate those 'fundamental principles of liberty and justice which lie at the base of all our civil and political institutions'? [as stated in *Hebert v. Louisiana* (1926)]. The answer surely must be 'no.' What the answer would have to be if the state were permitted after a trial free from error to try the accused over again or to bring another case against him, we have no occasion to consider. We deal with the statute before us and no other. The state is not attempting to wear the accused out by a multitude of cases with accumulated trials. It asks no more than this, that the case against him shall go on until there shall be a trial free from the corrosion of substantial legal error. This is not cruelty at all, nor even vexation in any immoderate degree. If the trial had been infected with error adverse to the accused, there might have been review at his instance, and as often as necessary to purge the vicious taint. A reciprocal privilege, subject at all times to the discretion of the presiding judge, has now been granted to the state. There is here no seismic innovation. The edifice of justice stands, its symmetry, to many, greater than before.

The Court Expands the Right to Counsel

Anthony Lewis

In 1962 Clarence Earl Gideon, a repeat felon, appealed his latest conviction to the U.S. Supreme Court. He complained that he had requested a lawyer at the time of his trial, but the trial judge had ignored the request. In short, Gideon believed he had been deprived of due process of law because he could not afford to pay for a lawyer.

In 1963 the U.S. Supreme Court heard the case of *Gideon v. Wainwright*. The case was remarkably like a prior case, *Betts v. Brady* (1943), in which the Supreme Court had determined that the Fourteenth Amendment's due process clause does not guarantee an attorney in a state criminal trial. However, Gideon's top-notch legal team prevailed. In an opinion authored by Justice Hugo Black (who had written the dissenting opinion in *Betts*), the prior case was overruled, and Gideon was granted a new trial. On retrial in Florida, a court-appointed local lawyer for Gideon hammered home the question of reasonable doubt with the jury. Gideon was found not guilty.

Anthony Lewis, a Pulitzer prize–winning journalist, was covering the Supreme Court at the time *Gideon* was decided. In 1963 Lewis won his second Pulitzer for his coverage of the Court. Shortly thereafter, he published the book *Gideon's Trumpet*, from which this selection is excerpted.

Lewis summarizes Justice Black's *Gideon* opinion, which eviscerated *Betts*. *Betts* had determined that the Sixth Amendment guarantee of the right to counsel is not so fundamental that it should be applied against the states by the Fourteenth Amendment. Yet Justice Black cited Supreme

Court case law, predating *Betts*, that emphasizes the importance of counsel. Aside from the legal precedent that should have reflected the fundamental nature of the right, Justice Black believed that "reason and reflection" demonstrate that a person without a lawyer cannot be assured a fair trial in the criminal justice system.

———————

[On March 18, 1963,] *Gideon v. Wainwright* was decided. There was no prior notice; there never is. The Court gives out no advance press releases and tells no one what cases will be decided on a particular Monday, much less how they will be decided. Opinion days have a special quality. The Supreme Court is one of the last American appellate courts where decisions are announced orally. The justices, who divide on so many issues, disagree about this practice, too. Some regard it as a waste of time; others value it as an occasion for descending from the ivory tower, however briefly, and communicating with the live audience in the courtroom. Techniques of opinion-reading vary, too. Justice [Felix] Frankfurter never looked at his text but would expound from memory; once Chief Justice [Earl] Warren irritatedly accused him of saying things that were not in the opinion. Others stick closely to the text, and some read brief summaries. Justice [Hugo] Black's technique seems to vary with the opinion; he gives fuller—and more emotional—treatment to those he regards as of particular importance.

The reading always begins with the most junior justice who has an opinion that day. On Monday, March 18th, that was the newest member of the Court, Justice [Arthur] Goldberg. . . .

[Eventually], in the ascending order of seniority, it was Justice Black's turn. He looked at his wife, who was sitting in the box reserved for the justices' friends and families, and said: "I have for announcement the opinion and judgment of the Court in Number One fifty-five, Gideon against Wainwright."

Justice Black leaned forward and gave his words the emphasis and the drama of a great occasion. Speaking very directly to the audience in the courtroom, in an almost folksy way, he told about Clarence Earl Gideon's case and how it had reached the Supreme Court of the United States.

"It raised a fundamental question," Justice Black said, "the rightness of a case we decided twenty-one years ago, Betts against Brady. When we granted certiorari in this case, we asked the lawyers on both sides to argue to us whether we should reconsider that case. We do reconsider Betts and Brady, and we reach an opposite conclusion."

By now the page boys were passing out the opinions. There were four—by Justices [William] Douglas, [Tom] Clark and [John] Harlan, in addition to the opinion of the Court. But none of the other three was a dissent. A quick look at the end of each showed that it concurred in the overruling of *Betts v. Brady*. On that central result, then, the Court was unanimous.

Justice Black began reading sections of his opinion. Since 1942, it said, the problem of the constitutional right to counsel in state criminal trials had been "a continuing source of controversy in both state and federal courts." . . . Justice Black, quoting briefly from the transcript of Gideon's trial, said Gideon had "conducted his defense about as well as could be expected from a layman." The way the whole case had developed, he said, was "strikingly like" what had happened in the Betts case. "Since the facts and circumstances of the two cases are so nearly indistinguishable, we think the *Betts v. Brady* holding, if left standing, would require us to reject Gideon's claim that the Constitution guarantees him the assistance of counsel."

Changing the Law

The rest of Justice Black's ten-page opinion was an assault on *Betts*. There was no attempt to show that overruling was required by developments in the two decades since the case was decided. It had been wrong to start with. Justice Black did not press his own theory that the Fourteenth Amendment incorporated the Bill of Rights verbatim. He accepted as the law, for purposes of this case, the [Justice Benjamin] Cardozo formulation that particular guarantees of the Bill of Rights "implicit in the concept of ordered liberty" had been "brought within the Fourteenth Amendment by a process of absorption" and thus had been made applicable to state proceedings.

"We accept," he wrote, "*Betts v. Brady*'s assumption, based as it was on our prior cases, that a provision of the Bill of Rights which is 'fundamental and essential to a fair trial' is made obligatory upon the states by the Fourteenth Amendment. We think the Court in *Betts* was wrong, however, in concluding that the Sixth Amendment's guarantee of counsel is not one of these fundamental rights. Ten years before *Betts v. Brady*, this Court [in *Powell v. Alabama* (1932)], after full consideration of all the historical data examined in *Betts*, had unequivocally declared that 'the right to the aid of counsel is of this fundamental character.' While the Court at the close of its *Powell* opinion did by its language, as this Court frequently does, limit its holding to the particular facts and circumstances of that case, its conclusions about the fundamental nature of the right to counsel are unmistakable."

Justice Black mentioned other early cases that had emphasized the importance of counsel, including his own 1938 opinion in *Johnson v. Zerbst*, construing the Sixth Amendment to require counsel in federal criminal trials, and concluded that *Betts* had made "an abrupt break" from these precedents.

"Not only these precedents but also reason and reflection," he wrote, "require us to recognize that in our adversary system of criminal justice, any person haled into court, who is too poor to hire a lawyer, cannot be assured a fair trial unless counsel is provided for him. This seems to us to be an obvious truth. Governments, both state and federal, quite properly spend vast sums of money to establish machinery to try defendants accused of crime. Lawyers to prosecute are everywhere deemed essential to protect the public's interest in an orderly society. Similarly, there are few defendants charged with crime, few indeed, who fail to hire the best lawyers they can get to prepare and present their defenses. That government hires lawyers to prosecute and defendants who have the money hire lawyers to defend are the strongest indications of the widespread belief that lawyers in criminal courts are necessities, not luxuries. The right of one charged with crime to counsel may not be deemed fundamental and essential to fair trials in some countries, but it is in ours."

The opinion came to an end without any mention of the difficult problems of the scope of the decision: what kinds of criminal cases it covered, if any apart from felonies; at what stage of the proceeding counsel was required; whether the decision applied to persons already in prison, so that those who had not had counsel must now be given new trials. All those questions were presumably left to be answered when raised specifically by later cases.

"The Court in *Betts v. Brady*," Justice Black concluded, "departed from the sound wisdom upon which the Court's holding in *Powell v. Alabama* rested. Florida, supported by two other states, has asked that *Betts v. Brady* be left intact. Twenty-three states, as friends of the Court, argue that *Betts* was 'an anachronism when handed down' and that it should now be overruled. We agree.

"The judgment is reversed and the cause is remanded to the Supreme Court of Florida for action not inconsistent with this opinion."

The Concurrences

Justice Douglas, while joining Justice Black's opinion, was not content to let the occasion pass without rearguing the old proposition that the Fourteenth Amendment incorporated all the Bill of Rights. "Unfortunately," he wrote in his concurring opinion, "it has never commanded a Court. Yet, happily, all constitutional questions are always open. And what we do today does not foreclose the matter."

Justice Clark did not accept the reasoning of Justice Black and the majority. In his concurring opinion he rested on the fact that the Court had already established an absolute right to counsel in cases involving the death penalty, even under *Betts v. Brady*. . . . "The Fourteenth Amendment requires due process of law for the deprival of 'liberty' just as for deprival of 'life,' and there cannot constitutionally be a difference in the quality of the process based merely upon a supposed difference in the sanction involved."

Justice Harlan also followed a legal path of his own. "I agree that *Betts v. Brady* should be overruled," he said, "but consider it entitled to a more respectful burial than has been accorded, at least"—he added in a respectful gesture to Justice Black's consistency of position for twenty-one years—"on the part of those of us who were not on the Court when that case was decided." Justice Harlan could not agree that *Betts* had broken with precedents looking toward an absolute right to counsel. *Powell v. Alabama* had rested on the special circumstances of the Scottsboro trial, and *Betts* had actually enlarged the right to counsel by indicating that it could exist even in a non-capital case where there were special circumstances. But the special-circumstance doctrine, Justice Harlan continued, had had "a troubled journey." It had been abandoned altogether in death [penalty] cases. In non-capital cases it had "continued to exist in form while its substance has been substantially and steadily eroded." The Court had not found a lack of special circumstances in any case heard and decided since *Quicksall v. Michigan*, in 1950. "The Court has come to recognize, in other words, that the mere existence of a serious criminal charge constituted in itself special circumstances requiring the services of counsel at trial. In truth the *Betts v. Brady* rule is no longer a reality.

"This evolution, however, appears not to have been fully recognized by many state courts, in this instance charged with the front-line responsibility for the enforcement of constitutional rights." . . . The opinion went on:

"To continue a rule which is honored by this Court only with lip service is not a healthy thing and in the long run will do disservice to the federal system. The special-circumstances rule has been formally abandoned in capital cases, and the time has now come when it should be similarly abandoned in non-capital cases, at least as to offenses which, as the one involved here, carry the possibility of a substantial prison sentence. (Whether the rule should extend to *all* criminal cases need not now be decided.) This indeed does no more than to

make explicit something that has long since been foreshadowed in our decisions."

The Long-Awaited End

That was the end of Clarence Earl Gideon's case in the
Supreme Court of the United States. . . .

Justice Black, talking to a friend a few weeks after the decision, said quietly: "When *Betts v. Brady* was decided, I never
thought I'd live to see it overruled."

The Court Establishes the Miranda Rights

Earl Warren

Several U.S. Supreme Court decisions of the 1960s changed how the role of an attorney is viewed in the context of due process for accused criminals. First, *Gideon v. Wainwright* guaranteed the right to an attorney in 1963. A year later a case called *Escobedo v. Illinois* held that accused criminals who are being interrogated must be permitted the chance to speak to a lawyer if they so desire. In 1966 the Court considered several cases together in which the police had obtained statements from suspects who were in custody, cut off from the outside world, and given no explanation of their rights. The statements were used against the defendants at trial, and the defendants were convicted.

The first case in the group involved Ernesto Miranda, a poor Mexican immigrant who suffered from severe sexual delusions. He was interrogated by two police officers for two hours without being advised that he had the right to an attorney. Miranda signed a confession, which was used against him at trial, and was convicted of kidnapping and rape.

Chief Justice Earl Warren, a former district attorney known for being tough on crime, authored the Court's decision in *Miranda v. Arizona* (1966). The opinion carefully examines the typical interrogation process, including excerpts from police instructional manuals. In view of the police procedures used, the Court crafted a list of warnings that the police have to give before they can start their interrogation tactics. These warnings have come to be known as the Miranda rights. Unless these warnings are issued, any statements obtained from the suspects cannot be used at trial.

Earl Warren, opinion, *Miranda v. Arizona*, 384 U.S. 436, June 13, 1966.

Without such a process, the Court believed, Constitutional protections against self-incrimination would be too easily trammeled.

The cases before us raise questions which go to the roots of our concepts of American criminal jurisprudence: the restraints society must observe consistent with the Federal Constitution in prosecuting individuals for crime. More specifically, we deal with the admissibility of statements obtained from an individual who is subjected to custodial police interrogation and the necessity for procedures which assure that the individual is accorded his privilege under the Fifth Amendment to the Constitution not to be compelled to incriminate himself. . . .

The constitutional issue we decide in each of these cases is the admissibility of statements obtained from a defendant questioned while in custody or otherwise deprived of his freedom of action in any significant way. In each, the defendant was questioned by police officers, detectives, or a prosecuting attorney in a room in which he was cut off from the outside world. In none of these cases was the defendant given a full and effective warning of his rights at the outset of the interrogation process. In all the cases, the questioning elicited oral admissions, and in three of them, signed statements as well which were admitted at their trials. They all thus share salient features—incommunicado interrogation of individuals in a police-dominated atmosphere, resulting in self-incriminating statements without full warnings of constitutional rights.

Examining Police Procedures

An understanding of the nature and setting of this in-custody interrogation is essential to our decisions today. The difficulty in depicting what transpires at such interrogations stems from the fact that in this country they have largely taken place incommunicado. . . .

A valuable source of information about present police practices, however, may be found in various police manuals and texts which document procedures employed with success in the past, and which recommend various other effective tactics. These texts are used by law enforcement agencies themselves as guides. It should be noted that these texts professedly present the most enlightened and effective means presently used to obtain statements through custodial interrogation. By considering these texts and other data, it is possible to describe procedures observed and noted around the country.

The [police] officers are told by the manuals that [in the words of Fred E. Inbau and John E. Reid] the "principal psychological factor contributing to a successful interrogation is privacy—being alone with the person under interrogation." . . .

To highlight the isolation and unfamiliar surroundings, the manuals instruct the police to display an air of confidence in the suspect's guilt and from outward appearance to maintain only an interest in confirming certain details. The guilt of the subject is to be posited as a fact. The interrogator should direct his comments toward the reasons why the subject committed the act, rather than court failure by asking the subject whether he did it. Like other men, perhaps the subject has had a bad family life, had an unhappy childhood, had too much to drink, had an unrequited desire for women. The officers are instructed to minimize the moral seriousness of the offense, to cast blame on the victim or on society. These tactics are designed to put the subject in a psychological state where his story is but an elaboration of what the police purport to know already—that he is guilty. Explanations to the contrary are dismissed and discouraged.

The texts thus stress that the major qualities an interrogator should possess are patience and perseverance. . . .

The manuals suggest that the suspect be offered legal excuses for his actions in order to obtain an initial admission of guilt. Where there is a suspected revenge-killing, for example, the interrogator may say [according to Inbau and Reid]:

Joe, you probably didn't go out looking for this fellow with the purpose of shooting him. My guess is, however, that you expected something from him and that's why you carried a gun—for your own protection. You knew him for what he was, no good. Then when you met him he probably started using foul, abusive language and he gave some indication that he was about to pull a gun on you, and that's when you had to act to save your own life. That's about it, isn't it, Joe?

Having then obtained the admission of shooting, the interrogator is advised to refer to circumstantial evidence which negates the self-defense explanation. This should enable him to secure the entire story. One [Inbau and Reid] text notes that "Even if he fails to do so, the inconsistency between the subject's original denial of the shooting and his present admission of at least doing the shooting will serve to deprive him of a self-defense 'out' at the time of trial."

Handling Uncooperative Suspects

When the techniques described above prove unavailing, the texts recommend they be alternated with a show of some hostility. One ploy often used has been termed the "friendly-unfriendly" or the "Mutt and Jeff" act. . . .

The interrogators sometimes are instructed to induce a confession out of trickery. The technique here is quite effective in crimes which require identification or which run in series. In the identification situation, the interrogator may take a break in his questioning to place the subject among a group of men in a line-up. [According to Charles E. O'Hara and Gregory L. O'Hara,] "The witness or complainant (previously coached, if necessary) studies the line-up and confidently points out the subject as the guilty party." Then the questioning resumes "as though there were now no doubt about the guilt of the subject.". . .

The manuals also contain instructions for police on how to handle the individual who refuses to discuss the matter entirely, or who asks for an attorney or relatives. The examiner is to concede him the right to remain silent. [As Inbau and Reid state,] "This usually has a very undermining effect. First of all, he is disappointed in his expectation of an unfavorable reaction on the part of the interrogator. Secondly, a concession of this right to remain silent impresses the subject with the apparent fairness of his interrogator." After this psychological conditioning, however, the officer is told to point out the incriminating significance of the suspect's refusal to talk:

> Joe, you have a right to remain silent. That's your privilege and I'm the last person in the world who'll try to take it away from you. If that's the way you want to leave this, O.K. But let me ask you this. Suppose you were in my shoes and I were in yours and you called me in to ask me about this and I told you, "I don't want to answer any of your questions." You'd think I had something to hide, and you'd probably be right in thinking that. That's exactly what I'll have to think about you, and so will everybody else. So let's sit here and talk this whole thing over. [Inbau and Reid]

Few will persist in their initial refusal to talk, it is said, if this monologue is employed correctly.

In the event that the subject wishes to speak to a relative or an attorney, the following advice is tendered:

> [T]he interrogator should respond by suggesting that the subject first tell the truth to the interrogator himself rather than get anyone else involved in the matter. If the request is for an attorney, the interrogator may suggest that the subject save himself or his family the expense of any such professional service, particularly if he is innocent of the offense under investigation. The interrogator may also add, "Joe, I'm only looking for the truth, and if you're telling the truth, that's it. You can handle this by yourself." [Inbau and Reid]

Protective Procedures Are Needed

From these representative samples of interrogation techniques, the setting prescribed by the manuals and observed in practice becomes clear. In essence, it is this: To be alone with the subject is essential to prevent distraction and to deprive him of any outside support. The aura of confidence in his guilt undermines his will to resist. He merely confirms the preconceived story the police seek to have him describe. Patience and persistence, at times relentless questioning, are employed. To obtain a confession [according to Inbau and Reid], the interrogator must "patiently maneuver himself or his quarry into a position from which the desired objective may be attained." When normal procedures fail to produce the needed result, the police may resort to deceptive stratagems such as giving false legal advice. It is important to keep the subject off balance, for example, by trading on his insecurity about himself or his surroundings. The police then persuade, trick, or cajole him out of exercising his constitutional rights.

Even without employing brutality, the "third degree" or the specific stratagems described above, the very fact of custodial interrogation exacts a heavy toll on individual liberty and trades on the weakness of individuals. . . .

It is obvious that such an interrogation environment is created for no purpose other than to subjugate the individual to the will of his examiner. This atmosphere carries its own badge of intimidation. To be sure, this is not physical intimidation, but it is equally destructive of human dignity. The current practice of incommunicado interrogation is at odds with one of our Nation's most cherished principles—that the individual may not be compelled to incriminate himself. Unless adequate protective devices are employed to dispel the compulsion inherent in custodial surroundings, no statement obtained from the defendant can truly be the product of his free choice. . . .

We have concluded that without proper safeguards the process of in-custody interrogation of persons suspected or accused of crime contains inherently compelling pressures which work to undermine the individual's will to resist and to compel him to speak where he would not otherwise do so freely. In order to combat these pressures and to permit a full opportunity to exercise the privilege against self-incrimination, the accused must be adequately and effectively apprised of his rights and the exercise of those rights must be fully honored.

It is impossible for us to foresee the potential alternatives for protecting the privilege which might be devised by Congress or the States in the exercise of their creative rule-making capacities. Therefore we cannot say that the Constitution necessarily requires adherence to any particular solution for the inherent compulsions of the interrogation process as it is presently conducted. Our decision in no way creates a constitutional straitjacket which will handicap sound efforts at reform, nor is it intended to have this effect. We encourage Congress and the States to continue their laudable search for increasingly effective ways of protecting the rights of the individual while promoting efficient enforcement of our criminal laws. However, unless we are shown other procedures which are at least as effective in apprising accused persons of their right of silence and in assuring a continuous opportunity to exercise it, the following safeguards must be observed.

The Right to Remain Silent

At the outset, if a person in custody is to be subjected to interrogation, he must first be informed in clear and unequivocal terms that he has the right to remain silent. For those unaware of the privilege, the warning is needed simply to make them aware of it—the threshold requirement for an intelligent decision as to its exercise. More important, such a warning is an absolute prerequisite in overcoming the inherent pressures of the interrogation atmosphere. It is not just the subnormal or woefully ignorant who succumb to an interrogator's imprecations, whether implied or expressly stated, that the interrogation will continue until a confession is obtained or that silence in the face of accusation is itself damning and will bode ill when presented to a jury. Further, the warning will show the individual that his interrogators are prepared to recognize his privilege should he choose to exercise it.

The Fifth Amendment privilege is so fundamental to our system of constitutional rule and the expedient of giving an adequate warning as to the availability of the privilege so simple, we will not pause to inquire in individual cases whether the defendant was aware of his rights without a warning being given. Assessments of the knowledge the defendant possessed, based on information as to his age, education, intelligence, or prior contact with authorities, can never be more than speculation; a warning is a clearcut fact. More important, whatever the background of the person interrogated, a warning at the time of the interrogation is indispensable to overcome its pressures and to insure that the individual knows he is free to exercise the privilege at that point in time.

The warning of the right to remain silent must be accompanied by the explanation that anything said can and will be used against the individual in court. This warning is needed in order to make him aware not only of the privilege, but also of the consequences of forgoing it. It is only through an awareness of these consequences that there can be any assurance of real understanding and intelligent exercise of the privilege. Moreover, this warning may serve to make the individual more acutely aware that he is faced with a phase of the adversary system—that he is not in the presence of persons acting solely in his interest.

The Right to Counsel

The circumstances surrounding in-custody interrogation can operate very quickly to overbear the will of one merely made aware of his privilege by his interrogators. Therefore, the right to have counsel present at the interrogation is indispensable to the protection of the Fifth Amendment privilege under the system we delineate today. Our aim is to assure that the individual's right to choose between silence and speech remains unfettered throughout the interrogation process. A once-stated warning, delivered by those who will conduct the interrogation, cannot itself suffice to that end among those who most require knowledge of their rights. A mere warning given by the interrogators is not alone sufficient to accomplish that end. . . . Even preliminary advice given to the accused by his own attorney can be swiftly overcome by the secret interrogation process. Thus, the need for counsel to protect the Fifth Amendment privilege comprehends not merely a right to consult with counsel prior to questioning, but also to have counsel present during any questioning if the defendant so desires.

The presence of counsel at the interrogation may serve several significant subsidiary functions as well. If the accused decides to talk to his interrogators, the assistance of counsel can mitigate the dangers of untrustworthiness. With a lawyer present the likelihood that the police will practice coercion is reduced, and if coercion is nevertheless exercised the lawyer can testify to it in court. The presence of a lawyer can also help to guarantee that the accused gives a fully accurate statement to the police and that the statement is rightly reported by the prosecution at trial.

An individual need not make a pre-interrogation request for a lawyer. While such request affirmatively secures his right to have one, his failure to ask for a lawyer does not constitute a waiver. No effective waiver of the right to counsel during interrogation can be recognized unless specifically made after the warnings we here delineate have been given. The accused who does not know his rights and therefore does not make a request may be the person who most needs counsel.

Accordingly we hold that an individual held for interrogation must be clearly informed that he has the right to consult with a lawyer and to have the lawyer with him during interrogation under the system for protecting the privilege we delineate today. As with the warnings of the right to remain silent and that anything stated can be used in evidence against him, this warning is an absolute prerequisite to interrogation. No amount of circumstantial evidence that the person may have been aware of this right will suffice to stand in its stead: Only through such a warning is there ascertainable assurance that the accused was aware of this right.

If an individual indicates that he wishes the assistance of counsel before any interrogation occurs, the authorities cannot rationally ignore or deny his request on the basis that the individual does not have or cannot afford a retained attorney. The financial ability of the individual has no relationship to the scope of the rights involved here. The privilege against self-incrimination secured by the Constitution applies to all individuals. The need for counsel in order to protect the privilege exists for the indigent as well as the affluent. In fact, were we to limit these constitutional rights to those who can retain an attorney, our decisions today would be of little significance. The cases before us as well as the vast majority of confession cases with which we have dealt in the past involve those unable to retain counsel. While authorities are not required to relieve the accused of his poverty, they have the obligation not to take advantage of indigence in the adminis- tration of justice. Denial of counsel to the indigent at the time of interrogation while allowing an attorney to those who can afford one would be no more supportable by reason or logic than the similar situation at trial and on appeal struck down in *Gideon v. Wainwright* (1963). . . .

An Attorney Will Be Appointed for a Poor Person

In order fully to apprise a person interrogated of the extent of his rights under this system then, it is necessary to warn him not only that he has the right to consult with an attor- ney, but also that if he is indigent a lawyer will be appointed to represent him. Without this additional warning, the ad- monition of the right to consult with counsel would often be understood as meaning only that he can consult with a lawyer if he has one or has the funds to obtain one. The warn- ing of a right to counsel would be hollow if not couched in terms that would convey to the indigent—the person most often subjected to interrogation—the knowledge that he too has a right to have counsel present. As with the warnings of the right to remain silent and of the general right to counsel, only by effective and express explanation to the indigent of this right can there be assurance that he was truly in a posi- tion to exercise it.

Once warnings have been given, the subsequent proce- dure is clear. If the individual indicates in any manner, at any time prior to or during questioning, that he wishes to re- main silent, the interrogation must cease. At this point he has shown that he intends to exercise his Fifth Amendment privilege; any statement taken after the person invokes his privilege cannot be other than the product of compulsion, subtle or otherwise. Without the right to cut off questioning, the setting of in-custody interrogation operates on the indi- vidual to overcome free choice in producing a statement after the privilege has been once invoked. If the individual states that he wants an attorney, the interrogation must cease until an attorney is present. At that time, the individual must have an opportunity to confer with the attorney and to have him present during any subsequent questioning. If the individual cannot obtain an attorney and he indicates that he wants one before speaking to police, they must respect his decision to remain silent.

This does not mean, as some have suggested, that each police station must have a "station house lawyer" present at all times to advise prisoners. It does mean, however, that if police propose to interrogate a person they must make known to him that he is entitled to a lawyer and that if he cannot afford one, a lawyer will be provided for him prior to any interrogation. If authorities conclude that they will not provide counsel during a reasonable period of time in which investigation in the field is carried out, they may refrain from doing so without violating the person's Fifth Amendment privilege so long as they do not question him during that time.

Waiver Is Possible

If the interrogation continues without the presence of an attorney and a statement is taken, a heavy burden rests on the government to demonstrate that the defendant knowingly and intelligently waived his privilege against self-incrimination and his right to retained or appointed counsel. This Court has always set high standards of proof for the waiver of constitutional rights, and we re-assert these standards as applied to in-custody interrogation. Since the State is responsible for establishing the isolated circumstances under which the interrogation takes place and has the only means of making available corroborated evidence of warnings given during incommunicado interrogation, the burden is rightly on its shoulders.

An express statement that the individual is willing to make a statement and does not want an attorney followed closely by a statement could constitute a waiver. But a valid waiver will not be presumed simply from the silence of the accused after warnings are given or simply from the fact that a confession was in fact eventually obtained. . . .

Moreover, where in-custody interrogation is involved, there is no room for the contention that the privilege is waived if the individual answers some questions or gives some information on his own prior to invoking his right to remain silent when interrogated.

Whatever the testimony of the authorities as to waiver of rights by an accused, the fact of lengthy interrogation or incommunicado incarceration before a statement is made is strong evidence that the accused did not validly waive his rights. In these circumstances the fact that the individual eventually made a statement is consistent with the conclusion that the compelling influence of the interrogation finally forced him to do so. It is inconsistent with any notion of a voluntary relinquishment of the privilege. Moreover, any evidence that the accused was threatened, tricked, or cajoled into a waiver will, of course, show that the defendant did not voluntarily waive his privilege. The requirement of warnings and waiver of rights is a fundamental with respect to the Fifth Amendment privilege and not simply a preliminary ritual to existing methods of interrogation. . . .

Proper Confessions Are Valid

Our decision is not intended to hamper the traditional function of police officers in investigating crime. When an individual is in custody on probable cause, the police may, of course, seek out evidence in the field to be used at trial against him. Such investigation may include inquiry of persons not under restraint. General on-the-scene questioning as to facts surrounding a crime or other general questioning of citizens in the fact-finding process is not affected by our holding. It is an act of responsible citizenship for individuals to give whatever information they may have to aid in law enforcement. In such situations the compelling atmosphere inherent in the process of in-custody interrogation is not necessarily present.

In dealing with statements obtained through interrogation, we do not purport to find all confessions inadmissible. Confessions remain a proper element in law enforcement. Any statement given freely and voluntarily without any compelling influences is, of course, admissible in evidence. The fundamental import of the privilege while an individual is in custody is not whether he is allowed to talk to the police without the benefit of warnings and counsel, but whether he can be interrogated. There is no requirement that police stop a person who enters a police station and states that he wishes to confess to a crime, or a person who calls the police to offer a confession or any other statement he desires to make. Volunteered statements of any kind are not barred by the Fifth Amendment and their admissibility is not affected by our holding today.

To summarize, we hold that when an individual is taken into custody or otherwise deprived of his freedom by the authorities in any significant way and is subjected to questioning, the privilege against self-incrimination is jeopardized. Procedural safeguards must be employed to protect the privilege, and unless other fully effective means are adopted to notify the person of his right of silence and to assure that the exercise of the right will be scrupulously honored, the following measures are required. He must be warned prior to any questioning that he has the right to remain silent, that anything he says can be used against him in a court of law, that he has the right to the presence of an attorney, and that if he cannot afford an attorney one will be appointed for him prior to any questioning if he so desires. Opportunity to exercise these rights must be afforded to him throughout the interrogation. After such warnings have been given, and such opportunity afforded him, the individual may knowingly and intelligently waive these rights and agree to answer questions or make a statement. But unless and until such warnings and waiver are demonstrated by the prosecution at trial, no evidence obtained as a result of interrogation can be used against him.

Due Process Protects the Rights of Juveniles

Abe Fortas

In 1964 Gerald Gault was a fifteen-year-old boy who had been in trouble with the law before. On the morning of June 8 he was picked up from his home by the police for allegedly making an obnoxious, indecent telephone call to a neighbor woman. The police left no notice at his home that Gerald was being held in police custody. His mother had to find out from a friend where her son was when she returned home from work.

On June 15 the juvenile court held a fairly informal hearing to determine the charges against Gerald. He was sentenced as a juvenile delinquent to serve six years in the Arizona State Industrial School. No appeal was available in a juvenile case.

The Gault family had to bring a writ of habeas corpus, a special legal proceeding by which citizens can inquire into the legality of a person's imprisonment, in an attempt to release Gerald from the detention school. However, there was no record or transcript of what had occurred at the juvenile hearing to present later at the habeas hearing; all that existed were the judge's testimony of what was said in the juvenile court versus the Gault family's version.

The case eventually went to the U.S. Supreme Court. In 1967 Justice Abe Fortas authored one of the most important decisions for juvenile rights in the history of the United States. He noted that an adult facing the same charges as those brought against Gault would have been subjected to a small fine and a maximum of two months in jail. Further, an adult would have been entitled to notice of the charges against him, the help of an attorney, the right to confront

Abe Fortas, opinion, *In re Gault et al.*, 387 U.S. 1, May 15, 1967.

witnesses testifying against him, the right to avoid self-incrimination, the right to a transcript of the original hearing, and the right to an appeal—all the essentials of due process in a criminal case. Fortas saw no reason why juveniles should be denied the basic due process rights that were guaranteed to adults. Gault's conviction was therefore overturned.

A year after authoring the *Gault* decision, Fortas was nominated to serve as chief justice of the Supreme Court. However, in the face of a financial scandal, he withdrew himself from consideration. In 1969, after decades of distinguished service in public and private legal positions, he resigned from the bench.

———————————

If Gerald [Gault] had been over 18, he would not have been subject to Juvenile Court proceedings. For the particular offense immediately involved, the maximum punishment would have been a fine of $5 to $50, or imprisonment in jail for not more than two months. Instead, he was committed to custody for a maximum of six years. If he had been over 18 and had committed an offense to which such a sentence might apply, he would have been entitled to substantial rights under the Constitution of the United States as well as under Arizona's laws and constitution. The United States Constitution would guarantee him rights and protections with respect to arrest, search and seizure, and pretrial interrogation. It would assure him of specific notice of the charges and adequate time to decide his course of action and to prepare his defense. He would be entitled to clear advice that he could be represented by counsel, and, at least if a felony were involved, the State would be required to provide counsel if his parents were unable to afford it. If the court acted on the basis of his confession, careful procedures would be required to assure its voluntariness. If the case went to trial, confrontation and opportunity for cross-examination would be guaranteed. So wide a gulf between the State's treatment of the adult and of the child requires a bridge sturdier than mere verbiage, and reasons more persuasive than cliche can provide. . . .

Notice of Charges

Appellants allege that the Arizona Juvenile Code is unconstitutional or alternatively that the proceedings before the Juvenile Court were constitutionally defective because of failure to provide adequate notice of the hearings. No notice was given to Gerald's parents when he was taken into custody on Monday, June 8, [1964]. On that night, when Mrs. Gault went to the Detention Home, she was orally informed that there would be a hearing the next afternoon and was told the reason why Gerald was in custody. The only written notice Gerald's parents received at any time was a note on plain paper from Officer Flagg [a deputy probation officer who was superintendent of the Detention Home where Gerald was being held] delivered on Thursday or Friday, June 11 or 12, to the effect that the judge had set Monday, June 15, "for further Hearings on Gerald's delinquency."

A "petition" was filed with the court on June 9 by Officer Flagg, reciting only that he was informed and believed that "said minor is a delinquent minor and that it is necessary that some order be made by the Honorable Court for said minor's welfare." The applicable Arizona statute provides for a petition to be filed in Juvenile Court, alleging in general terms that the child is "neglected, dependent or delinquent." The statute explicitly states that such a general allegation is sufficient, "without alleging the facts." There is no requirement that the petition be served and it was not served upon, given to, or shown to Gerald or his parents.

The Supreme Court of Arizona rejected appellants' claim that due process was denied because of inadequate notice. It stated that "Mrs. Gault knew the exact nature of the charge against Gerald from the day he was taken to the detention home." The court also pointed out that the Gaults appeared at the two hearings "without objection." The court held that because "the policy of the juvenile law is to hide youthful errors from the full gaze of the public and bury them in the graveyard of the forgotten past," advance notice of the specific charges or basis for taking the juvenile into custody and for the hearing is not necessary. It held that the appropriate rule is that "the infant and his parent or guardian will receive a petition only reciting a conclusion of delinquency. But no later than the initial hearing by the judge, they must be advised of the facts involved in the case. If the charges are denied, they must be given a reasonable period of time to prepare."

We cannot agree with the court's conclusion that adequate notice was given in this case. Notice, to comply with due process requirements, must be given sufficiently in advance of scheduled court proceedings so that reasonable opportunity to prepare will be afforded, and it must "set forth the alleged misconduct with particularity" [according to the report by the President's Commission on Law Enforcement and Administration of Justice]. It is obvious . . . that no purpose of shielding the child from the public stigma of knowledge of his having been taken into custody and scheduled for hearing is served by the procedure approved by the court below. The "initial hearing" in the present case was a hearing on the merits. Notice at that time is not timely; and even if there were a conceivable purpose served by the deferral proposed by the court below, it would have to yield to the requirements that the child and his parents or guardian be notified, in writing, of the specific charge or factual allegations to be considered at the hearing, and that such written notice be given at the earliest practicable time, and in any event sufficiently in advance of the hearing to permit preparation. Due process of law requires notice of the sort we have described—that is, notice which would be deemed constitutionally adequate in a civil or criminal proceeding. It does not allow a hearing to be held in which a youth's freedom and his parents' right to his custody are at stake without giving them timely notice, in advance of the hearing, of the specific issues that they must meet. Nor, in the circumstances of this case, can it reasonably be said that the requirement of notice was waived.

Right to Counsel

Appellants charge that the Juvenile Court proceedings were fatally defective because the court did not advise Gerald or his parents of their right to counsel, and proceeded with the hearing, the adjudication of delinquency and the order of commitment in the absence of counsel for the child and his parents or an express waiver of the right thereto. The Supreme Court of Arizona pointed out that "[t]here is disagreement [among the various jurisdictions] as to whether the court must advise the infant that he has a right to counsel." It noted its own decision in *Arizona State Dept. of Public Welfare v. Barlow* (1956), to the effect "that the parents of an infant in a juvenile proceeding cannot be denied representation by counsel of their choosing." It referred to a provision of the Juvenile Code which it characterized as requiring "that the probation officer shall look after the interests of neglected, delinquent and dependent children, including representing their interests in court." The court argued that "The parent and the probation officer may be relied upon to protect the infant's interests." Accordingly it rejected the proposition that "due process requires that an infant have a right to counsel." It said that juvenile courts have the discretion, but not the duty, to allow such representation; it referred specifically to the situation in which the Juvenile Court discerns conflict between the child and his parents as an instance in which this discretion might be exercised. We do not agree. Probation officers, in the Arizona scheme, are also arresting officers. They initiate proceedings and file petitions which they verify, as here, alleging the delinquency of the child; and they testify, as here, against the child. And here the probation officer was also superintendent of the Detention Home. The probation officer cannot act as counsel for the child. His role in the adjudicatory hearing, by statute and in fact, is as arresting officer and witness against the child. Nor can the judge represent the child. There is no material difference in this respect between adult and juvenile proceedings of the sort here involved. In adult proceedings, this contention has been foreclosed by decisions of this Court. A proceeding where the issue is whether the child will be found to be "delinquent" and subjected to the loss of his liberty for years is comparable in seriousness to a felony prosecution. The juvenile needs the assistance of counsel to cope with problems of law, to make skilled inquiry into the facts, to insist upon regularity of the proceedings, and to ascertain whether he has a defense and to prepare and submit it. The child "requires the guiding hand of counsel at every step in the proceedings against him" [*Powell v. Alabama* (1932)]. Just as in *Kent v. United States*, . . . we indicated our agreement with the United States Court of Appeals for the District of Columbia Circuit that the assistance of counsel is essential for purposes of waiver proceedings, so we hold now that it is equally essential for the determination of delinquency, carrying with it the awesome prospect of incarceration in a state institution until the juvenile reaches the age of 21.

During the last decade, court decisions, experts, and legislatures have demonstrated increasing recognition of this view. In at least one-third of the States, statutes now provide for the right of representation by retained counsel in juvenile delinquency proceedings, notice of the right, or assignment of counsel, or a combination of these. In other States, court rules have similar provisions. . . .

We conclude that the Due Process Clause of the Fourteenth Amendment requires that in respect of proceedings to determine delinquency which may result in commitment to an institution in which the juvenile's freedom is curtailed, the child and his parents must be notified of the child's right to be represented by counsel retained by them, or if they are unable to afford counsel, that counsel will be appointed to represent the child.

At the habeas corpus proceeding, Mrs. Gault testified that she knew that she could have appeared with counsel at the juvenile hearing. This knowledge is not a waiver of the right to counsel which she and her juvenile son had, as we have defined it. They had a right expressly to be advised that they might retain counsel and to be confronted with the need for specific consideration of whether they did or did not choose to waive the right. If they were unable to afford to employ counsel, they were entitled in view of the seriousness of the charge and the potential commitment, to appointed counsel, unless they chose waiver. Mrs. Gault's knowledge that she could employ counsel was not an "intentional relinquishment or abandonment" of a fully known right [*Johnson v. Zerbst* (1938)].

Confrontation, Self-Incrimination, Cross-Examination

Appellants urge that the writ of habeas corpus should have been granted because of the denial of the rights of confrontation and cross-examination in the Juvenile Court hearings, and because the privilege against self-incrimination was not observed. The Juvenile Court Judge testified at the habeas corpus hearing that he had proceeded on the basis of Gerald's admissions at the two hearings. Appellants attack this on the ground that the admissions were obtained in disregard of the privilege against self-incrimination. If the confession is disregarded, appellants argue that the delinquency conclusion, since it was fundamentally based on a finding that Gerald had made lewd remarks during the phone call to Mrs. Cook, is fatally defective for failure to accord the rights of confrontation and cross-examination which the Due Process Clause of the Fourteenth Amendment of the Federal Constitution guarantees in state proceedings generally.

Our first question, then, is whether Gerald's admission was improperly obtained and relied on as the basis of decision, in conflict with the Federal Constitution. For this purpose, it is necessary briefly to recall the relevant facts.

Confessions Must Be Viewed with Caution

Mrs. Cook, the complainant, and the recipient of the alleged telephone call, was not called as a witness. Gerald's mother asked the Juvenile Court Judge why Mrs. Cook was not present and the judge replied that "she didn't have to be present." So far as appears, Mrs. Cook was spoken to only once, by Officer Flagg, and this was by telephone. The judge did not speak with her on any occasion. Gerald had been questioned by the probation officer after having been taken into custody. The exact circumstances of this questioning do not appear but any admissions Gerald may have made at this time do not appear in the record. Gerald was also questioned by the Juvenile Court Judge at each of the two hearings. The judge testified in the habeas corpus proceeding that Gerald admitted making "some of the lewd statements . . . [but not] any of the more serious lewd statements." There was conflict and uncertainty among the witnesses at the habeas corpus proceeding—the Juvenile Court Judge, Mr. and Mrs. Gault, and the probation officer—as to what Gerald did or did not admit.

We shall assume that Gerald made admissions of the sort described by the Juvenile Court Judge, as quoted above. Neither Gerald nor his parents were advised that he did not have to testify or make a statement, or that an incriminating statement might result in his commitment as a "delinquent." . . .

This Court has emphasized that admissions and confessions of juveniles require special caution. In *Haley v. Ohio*, where this Court reversed the conviction of a 15-year-old boy for murder, Mr. Justice [William] Douglas said:

What transpired would make us pause for careful inquiry if a mature man were involved. And when, as here, a mere child—an easy victim of the law—is before us, special care in scrutinizing the record must be used. Age 15 is a tender and difficult age for a boy of any race. He cannot be judged by the more exacting standards of maturity. That which would leave a man cold and unimpressed can overawe and overwhelm a lad in his early teens. This is the period of great instability which the crisis of adolescence produces. A 15-year-old lad, questioned through the dead of night by relays of police, is a ready victim of the inquisition. Mature men possibly might stand the ordeal from midnight to 5 A.M. But we cannot believe that a lad of tender years is a match for the police in such a contest. He needs counsel and support if he is not to become the victim first of fear, then of panic. He needs someone on whom to lean lest the overpowering presence of the law, as he knows it, crush him. No friend stood at the side of this 15-year-old boy as the police, working in relays, questioned him hour after hour, from midnight until dawn. No lawyer stood guard to make sure that the police went so far and no farther, to see to it that they stopped short of the point where he became the victim of coercion. No counsel or friend was called during the critical hours of questioning. . . .

The privilege against self-incrimination is, of course, related to the question of the safeguards necessary to assure that admissions or confessions are reasonably trustworthy, that they are not the mere fruits of fear or coercion, but are reliable expressions of the truth. . . .

It would indeed be surprising if the privilege against self-incrimination were available to hardened criminals but not to children. The language of the Fifth Amendment, applicable to the States by operation of the Fourteenth Amendment, is unequivocal and without exception. . . .

"Delinquency" Is "Criminal"

Against the application to juveniles of the right to silence, it is argued that juvenile proceedings are "civil" and not "criminal," and therefore the privilege should not apply. It is true that the statement of the privilege in the Fifth Amendment, which is applicable to the States by reason of the Fourteenth Amendment, is that no person "shall be compelled in any criminal case to be a witness against himself." However, it is also clear that the availability of the privilege does not turn upon the type of proceeding in which its protection is invoked, but upon the nature of the statement or admission and the exposure which it invites. The privilege may, for example, be claimed in a civil or administrative proceeding, if the statement is or may be inculpatory.

It would be entirely unrealistic to carve out of the Fifth Amendment all statements by juveniles on the ground that these cannot lead to "criminal" involvement. In the first place, juvenile proceedings to determine "delinquency," which may lead to commitment to a state institution, must be regarded as "criminal" for purposes of the privilege against self-incrimination. To hold otherwise would be to disregard substance because of the feeble enticement of the "civil" label-of-convenience which has been attached to juvenile proceedings. Indeed, in over half of the States, there is not even assurance that the juvenile will be kept in separate institutions, apart from adult "criminals." In those States juveniles may be placed in or transferred to adult penal institutions after having been found "delinquent" by a juvenile court. For this purpose, at least, commitment is a deprivation of liberty. It is incarceration against one's will, whether it is called "criminal" or "civil." And our Constitution guarantees that no person shall be "compelled" to be a witness against himself when he is threatened with deprivation of his liberty—a command which this Court has broadly applied and generously implemented in accordance with the teaching of the history of the privilege and its great office in mankind's battle for freedom. . . .

Privilege Against Self-Incrimination Applies to Juveniles

We conclude that the constitutional privilege against self-incrimination is applicable in the case of juveniles as it is with respect to adults. We appreciate that special problems may arise with respect to waiver of the privilege by or on behalf of children, and that there may well be some differences in technique—but not in principle—depending upon the age of the child and the presence and competence of parents. The participation of counsel will, of course, assist the police, Juvenile Courts and appellate tribunals in administering the privilege. If counsel was not present for some permissible reason when an admission was obtained, the greatest care must be taken to assure that the admission was voluntary, in the sense not only that it was not coerced or suggested, but also that it was not the product of ignorance of rights or of adolescent fantasy, fright or despair.

The "confession" of Gerald Gault was first obtained by Officer Flagg, out of the presence of Gerald's parents, without counsel and without advising him of his right to silence, as far as appears. The judgment of the Juvenile Court was stated by the judge to be based on Gerald's admissions in court. Neither "admission" was reduced to writing and, to say the least, the process by which the "admissions" were obtained and received must be characterized as lacking the certainty and order which are required of proceedings of such formidable consequences. Apart from the "admissions," there was nothing upon which a judgment or finding might be based. There was no sworn testimony. Mrs. Cook, the complainant, was not present. The Arizona Supreme Court held that "sworn testimony must be required of all witnesses including police officers, probation officers and others who are part of or officially related to the juvenile court structure." We hold that this is not enough. No reason is suggested or appears for a different rule in respect of sworn testimony in juvenile courts than in adult tribunals. Absent a valid confession adequate to support the determination of the Juvenile Court, confrontation and sworn testimony by witnesses available for cross-examination were essential for a finding of "delinquency" and an order committing Gerald to a state institution for a maximum of six years.

CHAPTER THREE

Due Process and Civil Liberties

The Bill of Rights

Due Process Protects the Liberty of Contract

Rufus Peckham

In 1897 New York State passed a labor law that limited the number of hours a baker could work per week to sixty hours. A bakery in Utica, a small city in upstate New York, violated the law. In 1905 the matter reached the Supreme Court of the United States in the case of *Lochner v. New York*. Rufus Peckham, who served as an associate justice from 1896 to 1909, authored the opinion—an opinion that eventually made him infamous in the realm of constitutional jurisprudence. Peckham and his colleagues on the high court found the New York statute to be unconstitutional and struck it down. They reasoned that liberty of contract is part of an individual's liberty that is protected by the due process clause of the Fourteenth Amendment. The labor law violated this freedom by depriving employers and employees of the right to purchase and sell labor as they wished. Supporters of the labor law argued that it was essentially a health law meant to protect both bakers and consumers. However, Peckham's opinion indicated that the law was passed for "other motives." He concluded that supposed concern for the health of bakers was not a valid reason for the state to take paternalism to the point of interfering with a person's liberty. The *Lochner* ruling is an example of the Court's application of substantive due process, since it upheld a specific individual right against infringement by government legislation.

For the next thirty years the Supreme Court used the *Lochner* rationale to strike down various state statutes. The stricken statutes typically attempted to improve labor conditions or protect consumers, and the Court became known for

Rufus Peckham, opinion, *Lochner v. New York*, 198 U.S. 45, April 17, 1905.

promoting the theory of laissez-faire economics. However, in the 1930s the Court started to defer to the choices of the state legislatures with respect to economic matters. By 1955 the Court had abandoned *Lochner* and no longer used the substantive due process rationale to review economic regulations. However, in the 1960s the Court began to use substantive due process as the basis for protecting personal rights, such as the right to privacy.

The indictment, it will be seen, charges that the plaintiff in error violated the 110th section of article 8, chapter 415, of the Laws of 1897, known as the labor law of the state of New York, in that he wrongfully and unlawfully required and permitted an employee working for him to work more than sixty hours in one week. . . . The mandate of the statute, that 'no employee shall be required or permitted to work,' is the substantial equivalent of an enactment that 'no employee shall contract or agree to work,' more than ten hours per day; and, as there is no provision for special emergencies, the statute is mandatory in all cases. It is not an act merely fixing the number of hours which shall constitute a legal day's work, but an absolute prohibition upon the employer permitting, under any circumstances, more than ten hours' work to be done in his establishment. The employee may desire to earn the extra money which would arise from his working more than the prescribed time, but this statute forbids the employer from permitting the employee to earn it.

The Fourteenth Amendment Protects Liberty of Contract

The statute necessarily interferes with the right of contract between the employer and employees, concerning the number of hours in which the latter may labor in the bakery of the employer. The general right to make a contract in relation to his business is part of the liberty of the individual protected by the 14th Amendment of the Federal Constitution. Under that provision no state can deprive any person of life, liberty, or property without due process of law. The right to

purchase or to sell labor is part of the liberty protected by
this amendment, unless there are circumstances which exclude the right. There are, however, certain powers, existing
in the sovereignty of each state in the Union, somewhat
vaguely termed police powers, the exact description and limitation of which have not been attempted by the courts. Those
powers, broadly stated, and without, at present, any attempt
at a more specific limitation, relate to the safety, health,
morals, and general welfare of the public. Both property and
liberty are held on such reasonable conditions as may be imposed by the governing power of the state in the exercise of
those powers, and with such conditions the 14th Amendment
was not designed to interfere.

The state, therefore, has power to prevent the individual
from making certain kinds of contracts, and in regard to them
the Federal Constitution offers no protection. If the contract
be one which the state, in the legitimate exercise of its police
power, has the right to prohibit, it is not prevented from prohibiting it by the 14th Amendment. Contracts in violation of a
statute, either of the Federal or state government, or a contract to let one's property for immoral purposes, or to do any
other unlawful act, could obtain no protection from the Federal Constitution, as coming under the liberty of person or of
free contract. Therefore, when the state, by its legislature, in
the assumed exercise of its police powers, has passed an act
which seriously limits the right to labor or the right of contract in regard to their means of livelihood between . . . employer and employee, it becomes of great importance to
determine which shall prevail—the right of the individual to
labor for such time as he may choose, or the right of the state
to prevent the individual from laboring, or from entering into
any contract to labor, beyond a certain time prescribed by the
state. . . .

A Balance of Power

It must, of course, be conceded that there is a limit to the
valid exercise of the police power by the state. There is no
dispute concerning this general proposition. Otherwise the
14th Amendment would have no efficacy and the legislatures

of the states would have unbounded power, and it would be enough to say that any piece of legislation was enacted to conserve the morals, the health, or the safety of the people; such legislation would be valid, no matter how absolutely without foundation the claim might be. The claim of the police power would be a mere pretext, become another and delusive name for the supreme sovereignty of the state to be exercised free from constitutional restraint. This is not contended for. In every case that comes before this court, therefore, where legislation of this character is concerned, and where the protection of the Federal Constitution is sought, the question necessarily arises: Is this a fair, reasonable, and appropriate exercise of the police power of the state, or is it an unreasonable, unnecessary, and arbitrary interference with the right of the individual to his personal liberty, or to enter into those contracts in relation to labor which may seem to him appropriate or necessary for the support of himself and his family? Of course the liberty of contract relating to labor includes both parties to it. The one has as much right to purchase as the other to sell labor.

This is not a question of substituting the judgment of the court for that of the legislature. If the act be within the power of the state it is valid, although the judgment of the court might be totally opposed to the enactment of such a law. But the question would still remain: Is it within the police power of the state? and that question must be answered by the court.

The question whether this act is valid as a labor law, pure and simple, may be dismissed in a few words. There is no reasonable ground for interfering with the liberty of person or the right of free contract, by determining the hours of labor, in the occupation of a baker. There is no contention that bakers as a class are not equal in intelligence and capacity to men in other trades or manual occupations, or that they are not able to assert their rights and care for themselves without the protecting arm of the state, interfering with their independence of judgment and of action. They are in no sense wards of the state. Viewed in the light of a purely labor law, with no reference whatever to the question of health, we think that a law like the one before us involves neither the safety, the morals, nor the welfare, of the public, and that the interest of the public is not in the slightest degree affected by such an act. The law must be upheld, if at all, as a law pertaining to the health of the individual engaged in the occupation of a baker. It does not affect any other portion of the public than those who are engaged in that occupation. Clean and wholesome bread does not depend upon whether the baker works but ten hours per day or only sixty hours a week. The limitation of the hours of labor does not come within the police power on that ground.

It is a question of which of two powers or rights shall prevail—the power of the state to legislate or the right of the individual to liberty of person and freedom of contract. The mere assertion that the subject relates, though but in a remote degree, to the public health, does not necessarily render the enactment valid. The act must have a more direct relation, as a means to an end, and the end itself must be appropriate and legitimate, before an act can he held to be valid which interferes with the general right of an individual to be free in his person and in his power to contract in relation to his own labor. . . .

An Improper Regulation

We think the limit of the police power has been reached and passed in this case. There is, in our judgment, no reasonable foundation for holding this to be necessary or appropriate as a health law to safeguard the public health, or the health of the individuals who are following the trade of a baker. If this statute be valid, and if, therefore, a proper case is made out in which to deny the right of an individual, as employer or employee, to make contracts for the labor of the latter under the protection of the provisions of the Federal Constitution, there would seem to be no length to which legislation of this nature might not go. . . . We think that there can be no fair doubt that the trade of a baker, in and of itself, is not an unhealthy one to that degree which would authorize the legislature to interfere with the right to labor, and with the right of free contract on the part of the individual, either as employer or employee. In looking through statistics regarding all trades and occupations, it may be true that the trade of a baker does not appear to be as healthy as some other trades, and is also vastly more healthy than still others. To the common understanding the trade of a baker has never been regarded as an unhealthy one. Very likely physicians would not recommend the exercise of that or of any other trade as a remedy for ill health. Some occupations are more healthy than others, but we think there are none which might not come under the power of the legislature to supervise and control the hours of working therein, if the mere fact that the occupation is not absolutely and perfectly healthy is to confer that right upon the legislative department of the government.

It might be safely affirmed that almost all occupations more or less affect the health. There must be more than the mere fact of the possible existence of some small amount of unhealthiness to warrant legislative interference with liberty. It is unfortunately true that labor, even in any department, may possibly carry with it the seeds of unhealthiness. But are we all, on that account, at the mercy of legislative majorities? A printer, a tinsmith, a locksmith, a carpenter, a cabinetmaker, a dry goods clerk, a bank's, a lawyer's, or a physician's clerk, or a clerk in almost any kind of business, would all come under the power of the legislature, on this assumption. No trade, no occupation, no mode of earning one's living, could escape this all-pervading power, and the acts of the legislature in limiting the hours of labor in all employments would be valid, although such limitation might seriously cripple the ability of the laborer to support himself and his family. In our large cities there are many buildings into which the sun penetrates for but a short time in each day, and these buildings are occupied by people carrying on the business of bankers, brokers, lawyers, real estate, and many other kinds of business, aided by many clerks, messengers, and other employees. Upon the assumption of the validity of this act under review, it is not possible to say that an act, prohibiting lawyers' or bank clerks, or others, from contracting to labor for their employers more than eight hours a day would be invalid. It might be said that it is unhealthy to work more than that number of hours in an apartment lighted by artificial light during the working hours of the day; that the occupation of the bank clerk, the lawyer's clerk, the realestate clerk, or the broker's clerk, in such offices is therefore unhealthy, and the legislature, in its paternal wisdom, must, therefore, have the right to legislate on the subject of, and to limit, the hours for such labor; and, if it exercises that power, and its validity be questioned, it is sufficient to say, it has reference to the public health; it has reference to the health of the employees condemned to labor day after day in buildings where the sun never shines; it is a health law, and therefore it is valid, and cannot be questioned by the courts.

Not Just a Health Law

It is also urged, pursuing the same line of argument, that it is to the interest of the state that its population should be strong and robust, and therefore any legislation which may be said to tend to make people healthy must be valid as health laws, enacted under the police power. If this be a valid argument and a justification for this kind of legislation, it follows that the protection of the Federal Constitution from undue interference with liberty of person and freedom of contract is visionary, wherever the law is sought to be justified as a valid exercise of the police power. Scarcely any law but might find shelter under such assumptions, and conduct, properly so called, as well as contract, would come under the restrictive sway of the legislature. Not only the hours of employees, but the hours of employers, could be regulated, and doctors, lawyers, scientists, all professional men, as well as athletes and artisans, could be forbidden to fatigue their brains and bodies by prolonged hours of exercise, lest the fighting strength of the state be impaired. We mention these extreme cases because the contention is extreme. We do not believe in the soundness of the views which uphold this law.

On the contrary, we think that such a law as this, although passed in the assumed exercise of the police power, and as relating to the public health, or the health of the employees named, is not within that power, and is invalid. The act is not, within any fair meaning of the term, a health law, but is an illegal interference with the rights of individuals, both employers and employees, to make contracts regarding labor upon such terms as they may think best, or which they may agree upon with the other parties to such contracts. Statutes of the nature of that under review, limiting the hours in which grown and intelligent men may labor to earn their living, are mere meddlesome interferences with the rights of the individual, and they are not saved from condemnation by the claim that they are passed in the exercise of the police power and upon the subject of the health of the individual whose rights are interfered with, unless there be some fair ground, reasonable in and of itself, to say that there is material danger to the public health, or to the health of the employees, if the hours of labor are not curtailed. If this be not clearly the case, the individuals whose rights are thus made the subject of legislative interference are under the protection of the Federal Constitution regarding their liberty of contract as well as of person; and the legislature of the state has no power to limit their right as proposed in this statute. All that it could properly do has been done by it with regard to the conduct of bakeries, as provided for in the other sections of the act. These several sections provide for the inspection of the premises where the bakery is carried on, with regard to furnishing proper wash rooms and waterclosets, apart from the bake room, also with regard to providing proper drainage, plumbing, and painting; the sections, in addition, provide for the height of the ceiling, the cementing or tiling of floors, where necessary in the opinion of the factory inspector, and for other things of that nature; alterations are also provided for, and are to be made where necessary in the opinion of the inspector, in order to comply with the provisions of the statute. These various sections may be wise and valid regulations, and they certainly go to the full extent of providing for the cleanliness and the healthiness, so far as possible, of the quarters in which bakeries are to be conducted. Adding to all these requirements a prohibition to enter into any contract of labor in a bakery for more than a certain number of hours a week is, in our judgment, so wholly beside the matter of a proper, reasonable, and fair provision as to run counter to that liberty of person and of free contract provided for in the Federal Constitution.

Not Just a Consumer Protection Law

It was further urged on the argument that restricting the hours of labor in the case of bakers was valid because it tended to cleanliness on the part of the workers, as a man was more apt to be cleanly when not overworked, and if cleanly then his 'output' was also more likely to be so. What has already been said applies with equal force to this contention. We do not admit the reasoning to be sufficient to justify the claimed right of such interference. The state in that case would assume the position of a supervisor . . . , over every act of the individual, and its right of governmental interference with his hours of labor, his hours of exercise, the character thereof, and the extent to which it shall be carried would be recognized and upheld. In our judgment it is not possible in fact to discover the connection between the number of hours a baker may work in the bakery and the healthful quality of the bread made by the workman. The connection, if any exist, is too shadowy and thin to build any argument for the interference of the legislature. If the man works ten hours a day it is all right, but if ten and a half or eleven his health is in danger and his bread may be unhealthy, and, therefore, he shall not be permitted to do it. This, we think, is unreasonable and entirely arbitrary. When assertions such as we have adverted to become necessary in order to give, if possible, a plausible foundation for the contention that the law is a 'health law,' it gives rise to at least a suspicion that there was some other motive dominating the legislature than the purpose to subserve the public health or welfare. . . .

An Attempt at Control

It is impossible for us to shut our eyes to the fact that many of the laws of this character, while passed under what is claimed to be the police power for the purpose of protecting the public health or welfare, are, in reality, passed from other motives. We are justified in saying so when, from the character of the law and the subject upon which it legislates, it is apparent that the public health or welfare bears but the most remote relation to the law. The purpose of a statute must be determined from the natural and legal effect of the language employed; and whether it is or is not repugnant to the Constitution of the United States must be determined from the natural effect of such statutes when put into operation, and not from their proclaimed purpose. The court looks beyond the mere letter of the law in such cases.

It is manifest to us that the limitation of the hours of labor as provided for in this section of the statute under which the indictment was found, and the plaintiff in error convicted, has no such direct relation to, and no such substantial effect upon, the health of the employee, as to justify us in regarding the section as really a health law. It seems to us that the real object and purpose were simply to regulate the hours of labor between the master and his employees . . . , in a private business, not dangerous in any degree to morals, or in any real and substantial degree to the health of the employees. Under such circumstances the freedom of master and employee to contract with each other in relation to their employment, and in defining the same, cannot be prohibited or interfered with, without violating the Federal Constitution.

Due Process Prohibits Racial Segregation in Schools

Earl Warren

In 1896 the U.S. Supreme Court heard a case titled *Plessy v. Ferguson*. *Plessy* involved a Louisiana statute that required separate railroad cars for white and black passengers. One of the arguments against this practice was that the Fourteenth Amendment restricted the states from permitting such a law. The amendment in fact had been passed in the post–Civil War era to secure the rights of former slaves. Despite these arguments, the Court found that creating separate facilities for different races was an acceptable practice. As an example, the Court cited the fact that separate schools had been established for white and black children in many states. Without using the exact phrase, the Court authored the notion that "separate but equal" facilities—that is, separate facilities of equal quality—were constitutional.

Nearly sixty years later, the validity of segregated public schools became a direct question before the Court. In *Brown v. Board of Education* (1954), the Court declared that separate public educational facilities were inherently unequal. As a result, school segregation in various states violated the Fourteenth Amendment's guarantee of "equal protection."

In *Bolling v. Sharpe* (1954), a companion case to *Brown v. Board of Education*, the Court also considered a claim that segregated schools violated the Fifth Amendment's guarantee of due process. Because the schools in question in *Bolling* were situated in Washington, D.C., rather than in a state, the Fourteenth Amendment did not apply. However, the Fifth Amendment certainly applied to the federal district, and the Court struck down school segregation there as well.

Earl Warren, opinion, *Bolling v. Sharpe,* 347 U.S. 497, May 17, 1954.

Brown and *Bolling* were among the first cases that Earl Warren addressed as chief justice of the U.S. Supreme Court. His role as head of the Court came during a difficult time in America's history and at a point when the justices were deeply divided over how "activist" the Court should be. Yet Warren managed to write the *Brown* and *Bolling* opinions for a unanimous Court. In doing so he significantly changed race relations and the role of the Supreme Court in America. The decisions were a sign of events to come. The Warren Court went on to actively champion the rights of the individual in both the civil and criminal realms.

This case challenges the validity of segregation in the public schools of the District of Columbia. The petitioners, minors of the Negro race, allege that such segregation deprives them of due process of law under the Fifth Amendment. They were refused admission to a public school attended by white children solely because of their race. They sought the aid of the District Court for the District of Columbia in obtaining admission. That court dismissed their complaint. The Court granted a writ of certiorari before judgment in the Court of Appeals because of the importance of the constitutional question presented.

We have this day held that the Equal Protection Clause of the Fourteenth Amendment prohibits the states from maintaining racially segregated public schools. The legal problem in the District of Columbia is somewhat different, however. The Fifth Amendment, which is applicable in the District of Columbia, does not contain an equal protection clause as does the Fourteenth Amendment, which applies only to the states. But the concepts of equal protection and due process, both stemming from our American ideal of fairness, are not mutually exclusive. The "equal protection of the laws" is a more explicit safeguard of prohibited unfairness than "due process of law," and, therefore, we do not imply that the two are always interchangeable phrases. But, as this Court has recognized, discrimination may be so unjustifiable as to be violative of due process.

An Arbitrary Deprivation of Liberty

Classifications based solely upon race must be scrutinized with particular care, since they are contrary to our traditions and hence constitutionally suspect. As long ago as 1896, this Court declared [in *Gibson v. Mississippi* (1896)] the principle "that the Constitution of the United States, in its present form, forbids, so far as civil and political rights are concerned, discrimination by the General Government, or by the States, against any citizen because of his race." And in *Buchanan v. Warley*, the Court held that a statute which limited the right of a property owner to convey his property to a person of another race was, as an unreasonable discrimination, a denial of due process of law.

Although the Court has not assumed to define "liberty" with any great precision, that term is not confined to mere freedom from bodily restraint. Liberty under law extends to the full range of conduct which the individual is free to pursue, and it cannot be restricted except for a proper governmental objective. Segregation in public education is not reasonably related to any proper governmental objective, and thus it imposes on Negro children of the District of Columbia a burden that constitutes an arbitrary deprivation of their liberty in violation of the Due Process Clause.

In view of our decision that the Constitution prohibits the states from maintaining racially segregated public schools, it would be unthinkable that the same Constitution would impose a lesser duty on the Federal Government. We hold that racial segregation in the public schools of the District of Columbia is a denial of the due process of law guaranteed by the Fifth Amendment to the Constitution.

The Court Infers a Right to Privacy in the Fourteenth Amendment

Jerry Goldman

In 1973 the U.S. Supreme Court handed down one of the most controversial decisions in the nation's history, *Roe v. Wade*. Authored by Justice Harry Blackmun, the lengthy opinion considered medical evidence, constitutional arguments, and two impassioned oral presentations. In the end, the Court proclaimed that the right to privacy permitted a woman to obtain an abortion during the early stages of a pregnancy. Neither the right to privacy nor the issue of abortion are discussed anywhere in the Constitution. Rather, to reach the decision the Court used the doctrine of substantive due process under the Fourteenth Amendment to expand privacy rights.

The decision polarized the nation. Since 1973 Supreme Court justices essentially have been selected based on the "litmus test" of whether they would support *Roe*. Supporters of the decision have cited it to further expand the right to privacy. Critics of the decision have derided it on various grounds, ranging from its alleged lack of a constitutional basis to its moral implications.

Jerry Goldman is a political science professor at Northwestern University. He is also an author and the creator of the OYEZ Project, an online resource covering the Supreme Court, its various justices, and its constitutional decisions. In this article he summarizes the *Roe* case and its lingering controversy.

A merica's concerns over abortion—whether and under what circumstances it should be allowed—was catapulted into controversy on January 22, 1973. On that day, the U.S. Supreme Court declared unconstitutional, by a vote of 7-2, a Texas law prohibiting an abortion except for the purpose of saving a woman's life.

The decision—reached after two presentations before the court—invalidated abortion laws in 46 states. Few rulings have generated as much sustained criticism or fervent support as *Roe vs. Wade.*

The court declared:

- In the first three months of pregnancy, the abortion decision must be left to the woman and her physician.

- In the interest of protecting a woman's health, states may restrict but not prohibit abortions in the second three months, or trimester, of pregnancy.

- In the last three months of pregnancy, states may regulate—or even prohibit—abortions to protect the life of the fetus, except when medical judgment determines that an abortion is necessary to save the life of the mother.

A Shaky Start

"Jane Roe," later identified as Norma N. McCorvey, had sought an abortion in Texas, but since her life was not at risk, she was unable to obtain a legal one in that state. She eventually opted to have the child, and gave it up for adoption.

Newly minted lawyers Sarah Weddington and Linda Coffee decided to challenge the constitutionality of the Texas law, aiming to establish a new constitutional right allowing women to control their own bodies. Roe became the lead plaintiff in their class-action lawsuit, and they represented her.

The U.S. District Court for the Northern District of Texas declared Texas's abortion law unconstitutional but declined to grant injunctive relief to the plaintiffs. Roe et al appealed the court's injunctive ruling, while Wade cross-appealed, challenging the lower court's ruling that the law was unconstitutional.

First Argument at the Supreme Court

Weddington argued Roe's case before the Supreme Court. She faced seven, rather than nine, justices because two of them had recently retired. In fashioning her argument to justify striking down the Texas law, Weddington advanced many reasons, but none revealed the precise constitutional issues at stake.

When Justice Potter Stewart asked her to formulate her constitutional argument, Weddington reached into a grab bag of provisions. Although poised in delivery, Weddington seemed at a loss as to where in the U.S. Constitution she could peg her argument.

Weddington's opponent, Jay Floyd, started off on the wrong foot, and appeared to go downhill from there. He began, "It's an old joke, but when a man argues against two beautiful ladies like this, they are going to have the last word." None of the justices seemed amused.

The justices initially voted to strike down the Texas law, and Justice Harry A. Blackmun was chosen as the spokesman for the majority. His opinion, however, failed to persuade his colleagues on the court.

Moreover, some of the justices were miffed by the choice of Blackmun as spokesman.

Given the uncertainty among the justices, the testiness of their egos and the appointment of two new members—William H. Rehnquist and Lewis F. Power Jr.—the court decided to hear a second argument on *Roe vs. Wade*, and scheduled it for October 11, 1972.

Attorneys Argue the Case a Second Time

By then, Weddington had sharpened her argument. But so did her new opponent, Robert C. Flowers.

Weddington faced tough questions from the justices on the constitutional status of the unborn fetus. Flowers came under strong questioning from justices Stewart and Thurgood Marshall as to when life begins.

Once again, the majority-opinion assignment went to Blackmun.

His carefully crafted opinion failed to identify a specific U.S. constitutional guarantee to justify the court's ruling. Instead, he based the decision on the right to privacy protected by the due process clause of the Constitution's 14th Amendment. In effect, the court was enforcing a right that the Constitution did not specifically articulate.

A Wave of Criticism

Critics voiced their objections immediately. The dissenters— justices Rehnquist and Byron R. White—asserted what other people have frequently repeated since the decision: The court's judgment was directed by its own dislikes, not by any constitutional compass.

In the absence of any guiding principles, the critics declared, the justices in the majority simply substituted their views for the views of the state legislatures, whose abortion regulations they invalidated.

Academic critics also pounded the opinion, noting that the court had struck down legislation in the absence of any expressed constitutional provision or history.

A Key Question

Abortion-rights proponents had pegged their claims on a prominent Supreme Court decision, *Griswold v. Connecticut* (1965).

In *Griswold*, a seven-member court majority fashioned a right to marital privacy from several constitutional provisions, then used this privacy right to strike down a seldom-enforced state law that made the use of birth control devices a crime.

The abortion issue surfaced in the oral argument in the *Griswold* case.

Near the end of the second day of debate, Justice Hugo L. Black asked Professor Thomas Emerson, who sought to invalidate the Connecticut law, a question that foreshadowed the abortion maelstrom eight years later.

"With reference to all these things we've been talking about—privacy and so forth—would we invalidate all laws punishing people for bringing about abortions?"

Emerson responded that one issue (contraception) had nothing to do with the other (abortion).

Over a Quarter-Century Later

In the 25 years [plus] since the *Roe vs. Wade* decision, a bare majority of the Court continues to reaffirm the initial decision.

It did so most recently in 1992 in *Planned Parenthood vs. Casey*. At the same time, the justices have tolerated additional government restrictions on abortion procedures. It appears that divisions on the court still run deep.

Blackmun retired from the Court in 1994. In a rare television interview with ABC News, Blackmun insisted that *"Roe versus Wade* was decided . . . on constitutional grounds."

It was as if Blackmun were trying, by sheer force of will, to turn back 25 years' worth of stinging objections to the opinion he crafted.

Due Process Guarantees Fair Procedures, Not Substantive Rights

John Hart Ely

John Hart Ely was a constitutional scholar and Ivy League law school professor and dean. Among other notable accomplishments, he wrote a first draft of the brief for Clarence Earl Gideon, the accused felon in *Gideon v. Wainwright*, the case which established the right to counsel. He also served on the Warren Commission, which investigated the assassination of President John F. Kennedy, and later clerked for Chief Justice Earl Warren at the U.S. Supreme Court. He is most well known for his book *Democracy and Distrust: A Theory of Judicial Review*, which examines two conflicting theories of judicial review: "interpretivism" and "noninterpretivism" (also known as "activism"). Interpretivism holds that judges should apply a literal interpretation of the Constitution and the Bill of Rights. Noninterpretivism allows justices to go beyond the letter of the Constitution, even to the point of inferring rights that are not explicitly stated.

In the following excerpt from *Democracy and Distrust*, Ely explains that the due process clause of the Fourteenth Amendment lends itself to a noninterpretivist reading. However, he argues, such a reading has led to the emergence of the doctrine of substantive due process, the view that the amendment allows the Court to invalidate state laws based on their substance rather than the procedures they establish. Ely contends that this approach is flawed. Although he does not insist on a strictly interpretivist reading of the Fourteenth Amendment, he maintains that the amendment is intended to apply to criminal and civil procedures, not the substance of laws.

———————————

Constitutional provisions exist on a spectrum ranging from the relatively specific to the extremely open-textured. At one extreme—for example the requirement that the President "have attained to the Age of thirty five years"—the language is so clear that a conscious reference to purpose seems unnecessary. Other provisions, such as the one requiring that the President be a "natural born Citizen," may need a reference to historical usage so as to exclude certain alternative constructions—conceivably if improbably here, a requirement of legitimacy (or illegitimacy!) or non-Caesarian birth —but once that "dictionary function" is served, the provision becomes relatively easy to apply. Others, such as the First Amendment's prohibition of congressional laws "abridging the freedom of speech," seem to need more. For one thing, a phrase as terse as the others I have mentioned is here expected to govern a broader and more important range of problems. For another, and this may have something to do with the first, we somehow sense that a line of growth was intended, that the language was not intended to be restricted to its 1791 meaning. This realization would not faze Justice [Hugo] Black or most other interpretivists: the job of the person interpreting the provision, they would respond, is to identify the *sorts of evils* against which the provision was directed and to move against their contemporary counterparts. Obviously this will be difficult, but it will remain interpretivism. . . .

Interpretivism and the Eighth Amendment

Still other provisions, such as the Eighth Amendment's prohibition of "cruel and unusual punishments," seem even more insistently to call for a reference to sources beyond the document itself and a "framers' dictionary." It is possible to construe this prohibition as covering only those punishments that would have been regarded as "cruel and unusual" in 1791, but that construction seems untrue to the open-ended quality of the language. The interpretivist can respond as he did to the First Amendment, that even though it is true that the clause shouldn't be restricted to its 1791 meaning, it should be restricted to the general categories of evils at which the provision was aimed. If you pursue this mode of "interpretation" with regard to the Eighth Amendment, however—and the First Amendment case will come down to much the same thing—you'll soon find yourself, at worst, begging a lot of questions or, at best, attributing to the framers a theory that may be *consistent* with what they said but is hardly discoverable in their discussions or their dictionaries. But even admitting this, the disaster for the interpretivist remains less than complete. The Cruel and Unusual Punishment Clause does invite the person interpreting it to freelance to a degree, but the freelancing is bounded. The subject is punishments, not the entire range of government action, and even in that limited area the delegation to the interpreter is not entirely unguided: only those punishments that are in some way serious ("cruel") and susceptible to sporadic imposition ("unusual") are to be disallowed.

The Eighth Amendment does not mark the end of the spectrum, however. The Fourteenth Amendment . . . contains provisions that are difficult to read responsibly as anything other than quite broad invitations to import into the constitutional decision process considerations that will not be found in the language of the amendment or the debates that led up to it.

The Fourteenth Amendment Refers to Procedures

The provision most often cited in this connection is the Fourteenth Amendment's Due Process Clause, which provides that no state shall "deprive any person of life, liberty, or property, without due process of law." This is the clause to which the Court has tended to refer to "support" its sporadic ventures into across-the-board substantive review of legislative action. Its frequent invalidations of various sorts of worker protection provisions during the first third of this century cited the Due Process Clause as the basis of the Court's review authority. These cases are conventionally referred to under the head of *Lochner v. New York*, one of the earlier ones, and are now universally acknowledged to have been constitutionally improper—for obvious reasons by interpretivists, for somewhat less obvious ones by noninterpretivists. The Court's 1973 invalidation of the antiabortion laws of all fifty states in *Roe v. Wade* also relied on this clause. This "substantive due process" notion is widely accepted by commentators. For example Archibald Cox, who rejects *Roe* on other grounds, is not troubled by the interpretivist critique that nothing in the Constitution seems to address itself even remotely to the question of abortion. "I find sufficient connection in the Due Process Clause . . . The Court's persistent resort to notions of substantive due process for almost a century attests the strength of our natural law inheritance in constitutional adjudication, and I think it unwise as well as hopeless to resist it."

In fact this interpretation of the clause—as incorporating a general mandate to review the substantive merits of legislative and other governmental action—not only was not inevitable, it was probably wrong. The Fourteenth Amendment's Due Process Clause was taken from the identical provision, save that the earlier one applied to the federal government, of the Fifth Amendment. There is general agreement that the earlier clause had been understood at the time of its inclusion to refer only to lawful *procedures*. What recorded comment there was at the time of replication in the Fourteenth Amendment is devoid of any reference that gives the provision more than a procedural connotation. So far it all sounds quite straight forward, and more than a few commentators have concluded that it is crystal clear that the framers of the Fourteenth Amendment intended their Due Process Clause to reach only procedural questions. . . .

An Occasional Substantive Interpretation Intended?

Things are seldom so simple, however, particularly where the intent of the framers of the Fourteenth Amendment is concerned. Despite the procedural intendment of the original Due Process Clause, a couple of pre–Civil War decisions had construed the concept more broadly, as precluding certain substantive outcomes. One was *Wynehamer v. People* (1856), in which the New York Court of Appeals invalidated a prohibition law under a state due process guarantee identical in wording to that of the Fifth Amendment. Probably more notorious was *Dred Scott v. Sandford*, decided a year later, in which the Supreme Court voided the Missouri Compromise, Chief Justice [Roger] Taney delivering an "Opinion of the Court" (in whose theory only two of his brethren actually seem to have concurred) indicating in a passing reference that slaveholders had been denied due process. I am by no means suggesting that with these decisions the path of the law had been altered, that by the time of the Fourteenth Amendment due process had come generally to be understood as possessing a substantive component. Quite the contrary: *Wynehamer* and the *Dred Scott* reference were aberrations, neither precedented nor destined to become precedents themselves. (Other courts on which they were urged were quite acid in the judgment that they had misused the constitutional language by giving it a substantive reading.) I *am* suggesting that given these decisions—of at least one of which the framers of the Fourteenth Amendment were certainly well aware[1]—one cannot absolutely exclude the possibility that some of them, had the question been put, would have agreed that the Due Process Clause they were including could be given an occasional substantive interpretation.

The Language Itself Is Key

To put the question thus, however, is to lose the forest in the trees. It would be a mistake—albeit an understandable one in light of the excesses one witnesses at the other extreme—to dismiss "the intent of the framers" as beside any relevant point. Something that wasn't ratified can't be part of our Constitution, and sometimes in order to know what was ratified we need to know what was intended. (Unless we know whether "natural born" meant born to American parents on the one hand or born to married parents on the other, we don't

1. The Fourteenth Amendment was written in part to overrule *Dred Scott*.

know what the ratifiers thought they were ratifying and thus what we should recognize as the constitutional command.) Neither am I endorsing for an instant the nihilist view that it is impossible ever responsibly to infer from a past act and its surrounding circumstances the intentions of those who performed it. To frame the issue thus, however, is to bring to the fore what seems invariably to get lost in excursions into the intent of the framers, namely that *the most important datum bearing on what was intended is the constitutional language itself.* This is especially true where the legislative history is in unusual disarray—as is certainly the case with the Fourteenth Amendment—but the validity of the point extends further. In the first place, and this is also true of statutes and other group products, not everyone will feel called upon to place in the "legislative history" his precise understanding, assuming he has one, of the meaning of the provision for which he is voting or to rise to correct every interpretation that does not agree with his. One of the reasons the debate culminates in a vote on an authoritative text is to generate a record of just what there was sufficient agreement on to gain majority consent. Beyond that, however, the constitutional situation is special in a way that makes poring over the statements of members of Congress in an effort to amend or qualify the constitutional language doubly ill-advised. Congress's role in the process of constitutional amendment is solely, to use the Constitution's word, one of "proposing" provisions to the states: to become law such a provision must be ratified by three-quarters of the state legislatures. Now obviously there is no principled basis on which the intent of those voting to ratify can be counted less crucial in determining the "true meaning" of a constitutional provision than the intent of those in Congress who proposed it. That gets to include so many different people in so many different circumstances, however, that one cannot hope to gather a reliable picture of their intentions from any perusal of the legislative history. To complicate matters further, many of the records of the Fourteenth Amendment's ratification debates have not survived. Thus the only reliable evidence of what "the ratifiers" thought they were ratifying is the language of the provision they approved.

The debates (or other contemporary sources) can serve the "dictionary function" of resolving ambiguities, as in the natural born citizen case, but that function fulfilled, the critical record of what was meant to be proposed and ratified is what was proposed and ratified. . . .

Let us then turn, surely we are long overdue, to the language of the Due Process Clause. . . . There is simply no avoiding the fact that the word that follows "due" is "process." No evidence exists that "process" meant something different a century ago from what it does now—in fact . . . the historical record runs somewhat the other way—and it should take more than occasional aberrational use to establish that those who ratified the Fourteenth Amendment had an eccentric definition in mind. Familiarity breeds inattention, and we apparently need periodic reminding that "substantive due process" is a contradiction in terms—sort of like "green pastel redness."[2]

Due Process Has Been Constructed

One might assume that this doesn't matter, that it is revisionism for the sheer hell of it, since I've advertised that the Fourteenth Amendment *does* contain provisions—notably the Privileges or Immunities Clause—that contain the sort of invitation to substantive oversight that the Due Process Clause turns out to lack. Why should we care whether such oversight is called "substantive due process" or something else? The question is a fair one, but it turns out it may matter, because of the negative feedback effect the notion of substantive due process seems to be having on the proper function of the Due Process Clause, that of guaranteeing fair procedures. Until recently, the general outlines of the law of procedural due process were pretty clear and uncontroversial. The phrase "life, liberty or property" was read as a unit and given an open-ended, functional interpretation, which meant that the government couldn't seriously hurt you without due process of law. What process was "due" varied, naturally enough, with context, in particular with how seriously you

2. By the same token, "procedural due process" is redundant [author's comment].

were being hurt and what procedures would be useful and feasible under the circumstances. But if you were seriously hurt by the state you were entitled to due process. Over the past few years, however, the Court has changed all that, holding that henceforth, before it can be determined that you are entitled to "due process" at all, and thus necessarily before it can be decided what process is "due," you must show that what you have been deprived of amounts to a "liberty interest" or perhaps a "property interest." What has ensued has been a disaster, in both practical and theoretical terms. Not only has the number of occasions on which one is entitled to any procedural protection at all been steadily constricted, but the Court has made itself look quite silly in the process—drawing distinctions it is flattering to call attenuated and engaging in ill-disguised premature judgments on the merits of the case before it. (It turns out, you see, that whether it's a property interest is a function of whether you're entitled to it, which means the Court has to decide whether you're entitled to it before it can decide whether you get a hearing on the question whether you're entitled to it.) The line of decisions has been subjected to widespread scholarly condemnation, which suggests that sometime within the next thirty years we may be rid of it.

It is interesting to speculate on how it got started, though. As I indicated, the law of procedural due process was not in serious disarray, and the proposition that the government should be able seriously to hurt you without due process of law is hardly one that cries out for affirmation. Part of the explanation may lie in the recent resurrection of substantive due process. So long as *Lochner* lay in disrepute, and substantive due process was therefore as good as dead —that is, nonexistent or reduced to an essentially meaningless requirement that the government behave "rationally"—there was little risk in the premise that any serious governmental hurt should proceed by due process of law. That just meant people were typically entitled to fair procedures. But once "due process" is reinvested with serious *substantive* content, things get pretty scary and judges will naturally begin to look for ways to narrow the scope of their authority. The reaction is one that might have suggested that the error was in resurrecting substantive due process, but instead it seems to have meant that due process, properly so called, has been constricted.

Avoiding Shifting Standards

Even if the Due Process Clause were restricted to its proper role of guaranteeing fair procedures, that would not make it unimportant. For even if it lacks authority to second-guess the substantive policy being pursued, the Court can still render the implementation of that policy difficult by making the procedural requirements comparatively stringent. What's more, its judgment here is also somewhat untethered: asking what process is due will get the Court into some questions to which the Constitution does not begin to provide answers. This bothered Justice Black, perhaps most conspicuously in his 1970 dissent in *In re Winship*, where he refused to go along with the majority's holding that the Constitution required proof "beyond a reasonable doubt" in state criminal cases. The reasonable doubt standard does not appear anywhere in the Bill of Rights, so Justice Black, pursuing his "incorporation" theory,[3] refused to read it into the Fourteenth Amendment.

> The Bill of Rights, which in my view is made fully applicable to the States by the Fourteenth Amendment . . . does by express language provide for, among other things, a right to counsel in criminal trials, a right to indictment, and the right of a defendant to be informed of the nature of the charges against him. And in two places the Constitution provides for trial by jury, but nowhere in that document is there any statement that conviction of crime requires proof of guilt beyond a reasonable doubt. The Constitution thus goes into some detail to spell out what kind of trial a defendant charged with crime should have, and I believe that Court has no power to add to or subtract from the procedures set forth by the Founders. I realize that it is far easier to substi-

3. the theory that in light of the Fourteenth Amendment, the Bill of Rights applies to state governments as well as the federal government

tute individual judges' ideas of "fairness" for the fairness prescribed by the Constitution, but I shall not at any time surrender my belief that that document itself should be our guide, not our own concept of what is fair, decent, and right . . . As I have said time and time again, I prefer to put my faith in the words of the written Constitution itself rather than to rely on the shifting, day-to-day standards of fairness of individual judges.

Indeed he had said it "time and time again," and it is a valuable speech, but it rings less true in a procedural context. It is true that in deciding what process is due the Court will have to take into account various costs, principally in money and time, that the Constitution will not help us assess. But that is hardly unique to due process. And the questions that are relevant here—how seriously the complainant is being hurt and how much it will cost to give him a more effective hearing—are importantly different from the question the Court makes relevant in "substantive due process" decisions like *Lochner* and *Roe*, namely how desirable or important the substantive policy the legislature has decided to follow is. Moreover, and here the parallel to the Cruel and Unusual Punishment Clause is extended, the decisions here are made in limited compass. The question is what procedures are required to treat the complainant this way, not whether the complainant can be treated this way at all: it's an important and difficult question, but a more limited one. Finally, what procedures are needed fairly to make what decisions are the sorts of questions lawyers and judges are good at. (Observe a lawyer on a committee with nonlawyers and see what role he or she ends up playing.) Thus the delegation, though assuredly it is that, is a limited and not terribly frightening one.

Due Process Prohibits Government Control of Personal Relationships

Anthony Kennedy

In 1986 the U.S. Supreme Court heard a case called *Bowers v. Hardwick*. Police had entered the bedroom of Michael Hardwick with a search warrant, which was unrelated to the case that later developed. They found Hardwick engaged in consensual homosexual relations with another adult male and arrested him under a Georgia sodomy law. Hardwick challenged the constitutionality of the law. However, the Court was hesitant to extend the right to privacy that was discussed in *Roe v. Wade* and declared that there was no "fundamental right to engage in homosexual sodomy."

Subsequently, several states took their sodomy laws off the books. In the remaining states, it appeared that sodomy laws, which were written to cover heterosexual and homosexual sodomy, were only being enforced against homosexuals.

Seventeen years after *Bowers*, the Supreme Court heard *Lawrence v. Texas*. The facts of the case were nearly identical to those of *Bowers*. Nevertheless, in an opinion authored by Justice Anthony Kennedy, the Court specifically overruled *Bowers*. Justice Kennedy noted that cases had evolved to protect heterosexuals' personal decisions relating to marriage, procreation, contraception, family relationships, child rearing, and education. The Court reasoned that the ability to make decisions regarding such intimate matters should not be denied to people in homosexual relationships. Such decisions are a form of liberty protected by the due process clause of the Fourteenth Amendment.

Anthony Kennedy, opinion, *Lawrence v. Texas,* 539 U.S. 558, June 26, 2003.

Justice Kennedy was President Ronald Reagan's third choice to fill a single vacancy on the Supreme Court—after Robert Bork's conservative ideology and Douglas Ginsburg's admission of marijuana use ended their hopes of confirmation. Yet the selection of Kennedy proved a pivotal one. Kennedy is often able to craft a consensus between the Court's conservative and liberal coalitions.

The question before the Court is the validity of a Texas statute making it a crime for two persons of the same sex to engage in certain intimate sexual conduct.

In Houston, Texas, officers of the Harris County Police Department were dispatched to a private residence in response to a reported weapons disturbance. They entered an apartment where one of the petitioners, John Geddes Lawrence, resided. The right of the police to enter does not seem to have been questioned. The officers observed Lawrence and another man, Tyron Garner, engaging in a sexual act. The two petitioners were arrested, held in custody over night, and charged and convicted before a Justice of the Peace. . . .

The applicable state law is Tex. Penal Code Ann. sect. 21.06(a) (2003). It provides: "A person commits an offense if he engages in deviate sexual intercourse with another individual of the same sex." . . .

The petitioners were adults at the time of the alleged offense. Their conduct was in private and consensual.

Comparisons with *Bowers*

We conclude the case should be resolved by determining whether the petitioners were free as adults to engage in the private conduct in the exercise of their liberty under the Due Process Clause of the Fourteenth Amendment to the Constitution. For this inquiry we deem it necessary to reconsider the Court's holding in *Bowers* [*v. Hardwick*].

The facts in *Bowers* had some similarities to the instant case. A police officer, whose right to enter seems not to have been in question, observed Hardwick, in his own bedroom, engaging in intimate sexual conduct with another adult male. The conduct was in violation of a Georgia statute making it a criminal offense to engage in sodomy. One difference between the two cases is that the Georgia statute prohibited the conduct whether or not the participants were of the same sex, while the Texas statute, as we have seen, applies only to participants of the same sex. Hardwick was not prosecuted, but he brought an action in federal court to declare the state statute invalid. He alleged he was a practicing homosexual and that the criminal prohibition violated rights guaranteed to him by the Constitution. The Court . . . sustained the Georgia law. . . .

Government Should Not Control Personal Relationships

The Court began its substantive discussion in *Bowers* as follows: "The issue presented is whether the Federal Constitution confers a fundamental right upon homosexuals to engage in sodomy and hence invalidates the laws of the many States that still make such conduct illegal and have done so for a very long time." That statement, we now conclude, discloses the Court's own failure to appreciate the extent of the liberty at stake. To say that the issue in *Bowers* was simply the right to engage in certain sexual conduct demeans the claim the individual put forward, just as it would demean a married couple were it to be said marriage is simply about the right to have sexual intercourse. The laws involved in *Bowers* and here are, to be sure, statutes that purport to do no more than prohibit a particular sexual act. Their penalties and purposes, though, have more far-reaching consequences, touching upon the most private human conduct, sexual behavior, and in the most private of places, the home. The statutes do seek to control a personal relationship that, whether or not entitled to formal recognition in the law, is within the liberty of persons to choose without being punished as criminals.

This, as a general rule, should counsel against attempts by the State, or a court, to define the meaning of the relationship or to set its boundaries absent injury to a person or abuse of an institution the law protects. It suffices for us to acknowledge that adults may choose to enter upon this relationship in the confines of their homes and their own private lives and still retain their dignity as free persons. When sexuality finds overt expression in intimate conduct with another person, the conduct can be but one element in a personal bond that is more enduring. The liberty protected by the Constitution allows homosexual persons the right to make this choice. . . .

It must be acknowledged, of course, that the Court in *Bowers* was making the broader point that for centuries there have been powerful voices to condemn homosexual conduct as immoral. The condemnation has been shaped by religious beliefs, conceptions of right and acceptable behavior, and respect for the traditional family. For many persons these are not trivial concerns but profound and deep convictions accepted as ethical and moral principles to which they aspire and which thus determine the course of their lives. These considerations do not answer the question before us, however. The issue is whether the majority may use the power of the State to enforce these views on the whole society through operation of the criminal law. "Our obligation is to define the liberty of all, not to mandate our own moral code." *Planned Parenthood of Southeastern Pa.* v. *Casey*, (1992). . . .

The Right to Make Personal Choices

Two principal cases decided after *Bowers* cast its holding into . . . doubt. In *Planned Parenthood of Southeastern Pa.* v. *Casey* (1992), the Court reaffirmed the substantive force of the liberty protected by the Due Process Clause. The *Casey* decision again confirmed that our laws and tradition afford constitutional protection to personal decisions relating to marriage, procreation, contraception, family relationships, child rearing, and education. In explaining the respect the Constitution demands for the autonomy of the person in making these choices, we stated as follows:

These matters, involving the most intimate and personal choices a person may make in a lifetime, choices central to personal dignity and autonomy, are central to the liberty protected by the Fourteenth Amendment.

> At the heart of liberty is the right to define one's own
> concept of existence, of meaning, of the universe, and
> of the mystery of human life. Beliefs about these mat-
> ters could not define the attributes of personhood were
> they formed under compulsion of the State.

Persons in a homosexual relationship may seek autonomy
for these purposes, just as heterosexual persons do. The decision in *Bowers* would deny them this right.

The second post-*Bowers* case of principal relevance is
Romer v. Evans (1996). There the Court struck down class-
based legislation directed at homosexuals as a violation of
the Equal Protection Clause. . . .

Equality of treatment and the due process right to demand respect for conduct protected by the substantive guarantee of liberty are linked in important respects, and a
decision on the latter point advances both interests. . . . When
homosexual conduct is made criminal by the law of the State,
that declaration in and of itself is an invitation to subject homosexual persons to discrimination both in the public and in
the private spheres. The central holding of *Bowers* has been
brought in question by this case, and it should be addressed.
Its continuance as precedent demeans the lives of homosexual persons. . . .

Bowers Should Be Overruled

The foundations of *Bowers* have sustained serious erosion
from our recent decisions in *Casey* and *Romer*. When our
precedent has been thus weakened, criticism from other
sources is of greater significance. In the United States, criticism of *Bowers* has been substantial and continuing, disap-
proving of its reasoning in all respects. . . . The courts of five
different States have declined to follow it in interpreting provisions in their own state constitutions parallel to the Due
Process Clause of the Fourteenth Amendment. . . .

To the extent *Bowers* relied on values we share with a
wider civilization, it should be noted that the reasoning and
holding in *Bowers* have been rejected elsewhere. The Euro-
pean Court of Human Rights has [not] followed *Bowers*. . . .

Other nations, too, have taken action consistent with an affirmation of the protected right of homosexual adults to engage in intimate, consensual conduct. The right the petitioners seek in this case has been accepted as an integral part of human freedom in many other countries. There has been no showing that in this country the governmental interest in circumscribing personal choice is somehow more legitimate or urgent. . . .

In *Casey* we noted that when a Court is asked to overrule a precedent recognizing a constitutional liberty interest, individual or societal reliance on the existence of that liberty cautions with particular strength against reversing course. The holding in *Bowers*, however, has not induced detrimental reliance comparable to some instances where recognized individual rights are involved. Indeed, there has been no individual or societal reliance on *Bowers* of the sort that could counsel against overturning its holding once there are compelling reasons to do so. *Bowers* itself causes uncertainty, for the precedents before and after its issuance contradict its central holding.

The rationale of *Bowers* does not withstand careful analysis. In his dissenting opinion in *Bowers* Justice [John Paul] Stevens came to these conclusions:

> Our prior cases make two propositions abundantly clear. First, the fact that the governing majority in a State has traditionally viewed a particular practice as immoral is not a sufficient reason for upholding a law prohibiting the practice; neither history nor tradition could save a law prohibiting miscegenation [interracial marriage] from constitutional attack. Second, individual decisions by married persons, concerning the intimacies of their physical relationship, even when not intended to produce offspring, are a form of "liberty" protected by the Due Process Clause of the Fourteenth Amendment. Moreover, this protection extends to intimate choices by unmarried as well as married persons.

Justice Stevens' analysis, in our view, should have been controlling in *Bowers* and should control here.

Bowers was not correct when it was decided, and it is not correct today. It ought not to remain binding precedent. *Bowers* v. *Hardwick* should be and now is overruled.

Government Cannot Control Private Consensual Sexual Conduct

The present case does not involve minors. It does not involve persons who might be injured or coerced or who are situated in relationships where consent might not easily be refused. It does not involve public conduct or prostitution. It does not involve whether the government must give formal recognition to any relationship that homosexual persons seek to enter. The case does involve two adults who, with full and mutual consent from each other, engaged in sexual practices common to a homosexual lifestyle. The petitioners are entitled to respect for their private lives. The State cannot demean their existence or control their destiny by making their private sexual conduct a crime. Their right to liberty under the Due Process Clause gives them the full right to engage in their conduct without intervention of the government. [As the Court stated in *Casey,*] "It is a promise of the Constitution that there is a realm of personal liberty which the government may not enter." The Texas statute furthers no legitimate state interest which can justify its intrusion into the personal and private life of the individual.

Had those who drew and ratified the Due Process Clauses of the Fifth Amendment or the Fourteenth Amendment known the components of liberty in its manifold possibilities, they might have been more specific. They did not presume to have this insight. They knew times can blind us to certain truths and later generations can see that laws once thought necessary and proper in fact serve only to oppress. As the Constitution endures, persons in every generation can invoke its principles in their own search for greater freedom.

CHAPTER FOUR

Current Issues
and Perspectives

The Bill of Rights

"Enemy Combatants" Are Entitled to Due Process Protections

Sandra Day O'Connor

Shortly after the terrorist attacks against the United States on September 11, 2001, President George W. Bush sent U.S. armed forces into Afghanistan to quash the Taliban regime, which had supported the group believed to be responsible for the attacks. During the fighting, an American citizen named Yaser Esam Hamdi was apprehended in Afghanistan by members of the Northern Alliance, a native coalition fighting the Taliban. Hamdi allegedly was affiliated with a Taliban military unit. The Northern Alliance subsequently turned Hamdi over to the U.S. military. The military interrogated him in Afghanistan, transferred him to the U.S. Naval Base in Guantánamo Bay, Cuba, and eventually transferred him to a naval brig in the United States.

The United States government held Hamdi as an "enemy combatant" without formal charges or proceedings and without an attorney. In June 2002 Hamdi's father filed a petition for a writ of habeas corpus. The petition sought, among other things, Hamdi's release and a declaration that Hamdi was being held in violation of his Fifth and Fourteenth Amendment due process rights.

In June 2004 the U.S. Supreme Court issued a decision in the *Hamdi v. Rumsfeld* case. The case resulted in a plurality opinion—an opinion that does not carry a majority on all the issues—authored by Justice Sandra Day O'Connor. Justice O'Connor and three other justices held that Hamdi's initial detention was legal but that due process requires a meaningful opportunity for Hamdi to contest his "enemy

Sandra Day O'Connor, opinion, *Hamdi v. Rumsfeld,* No. 03-6696, June 28, 2004.

combatant" status. Two other justices found that the detention was not authorized to start with but joined with part of the O'Connor opinion solely to indicate that Hamdi deserved a meaningful opportunity to contest his status.

Part of O'Connor's plurality opinion applies a test from the Court's 1976 *Mathews v. Eldridge* case. The test determines the procedures necessary to ensure that a citizen is not deprived of life, liberty, or property without due process of law when there are serious competing interests at stake. First, the Court must weigh the private interest against the government's interest. In doing so the Court takes into consideration the governmental function at issue and the burden the government would face to provide any greater process. Then, a "judicious balancing" of the interests is done by weighing the risk of an improper result if less process is used against the "probable value, if any" of using more procedural safeguards.

The private interest in *Hamdi* was "the fundamental nature of a citizen's right to be free from involuntary confinement by his own government without due process of law." The government's interest was the "weighty and sensitive governmental interests in ensuring that those who have in fact fought with the enemy during a war do not return to battle against the United States." The weighing and balancing of these interests is discussed in the excerpt that follows.

Striking the proper constitutional balance here is of great importance to the Nation during this period of ongoing combat. But it is equally vital that our calculus not give short shrift to the values that this country holds dear or to the privilege that is American citizenship. It is during our most challenging and uncertain moments that our Nation's commitment to due process is most severely tested; and it is in those times that we must preserve our commitment at home to the principles for which we fight abroad. . . .

Finding a Balance

With due recognition of these competing concerns, we believe that neither the process proposed by the Government nor the process apparently envisioned by the District Court below strikes the proper constitutional balance when a United States citizen is detained in the United States as an enemy combatant. That is [quoting the Court's ruling in *Mathews* v. *Eldridge* (1976)], "the risk of erroneous deprivation" of a detainee's liberty interest is unacceptably high under the Government's proposed rule, while some of the "additional or substitute procedural safeguards" suggested by the District Court are unwarranted in light of their limited "probable value" and the burdens they may impose on the military in such cases.

We therefore hold that a citizen-detainee seeking to challenge his classification as an enemy combatant must receive notice of the factual basis for his classification, and a fair opportunity to rebut the Government's factual assertions before a neutral decisionmaker. . . . "For more than a century the central meaning of procedural due process has been clear: 'Parties whose rights are to be affected are entitled to be heard; and in order that they may enjoy that right they must first be notified.' It is equally fundamental that the right to notice and an opportunity to be heard 'must be granted at a meaningful time and in a meaningful manner.'" *Fuentes* v. *Shevin*, (1972) (quoting *Baldwin* v. *Hale*, (1864) [et al.]). These essential constitutional promises may not be eroded.

At the same time, the exigencies of the circumstances may demand that, aside from these core elements, enemy combatant proceedings may be tailored to alleviate their uncommon potential to burden the Executive at a time of ongoing military conflict. Hearsay, for example, may need to be accepted as the most reliable available evidence from the Government in such a proceeding. Likewise, the Constitution would not be offended by a presumption in favor of the Government's evidence, so long as that presumption remained a rebuttable one and fair opportunity for rebuttal were provided. Thus, once the Government puts forth credible evidence that the habeas petitioner meets the enemy-combatant criteria, the onus could shift to the petitioner to rebut that evidence with more persuasive evidence that he falls outside the criteria. A burden-shifting scheme of this sort would meet the goal of ensuring that the errant tourist, embedded journalist, or local aid worker has a chance to prove military error while giving due regard to the Executive once it has put forth meaningful support for its conclusion that the detainee is in fact an enemy combatant. In the words of *Mathews*, process of this sort would sufficiently address the "risk of erroneous deprivation" of a detainee's liberty interest while eliminating certain procedures that have questionable additional value in light of the burden on the Government.

Warmaking Powers Are Left Intact

We think it unlikely that this basic process will have the dire impact on the central functions of warmaking that the Government forecasts. The parties agree that initial captures on the battlefield need not receive the process we have discussed here; that process is due only when the determination is made to *continue* to hold those who have been seized. The Government has made clear in its briefing that documentation regarding battlefield detainees already is kept in the ordinary course of military affairs. Any factfinding imposition created by requiring a knowledgeable affiant to summarize these records to an independent tribunal is a minimal one. Likewise, arguments that military officers ought not have to wage war under the threat of litigation lose much of their steam when factual disputes at enemy-combatant hearings are limited to the alleged combatant's acts. This focus meddles little, if at all, in the strategy or conduct of war, inquiring only into the appropriateness of continuing to detain an individual claimed to have taken up arms against the United States. While we accord the greatest respect and consideration to the judgments of military authorities in matters relating to the actual prosecution of a war, and recognize that the scope of that discretion necessarily is wide, it does not infringe on the core role of the military for the courts to exercise their own time-honored and constitutionally mandated roles of reviewing and resolving claims like those presented here. . . .

In sum, while the full protections that accompany challenges to detentions in other settings may prove unworkable and inappropriate in the enemy-combatant setting, the threats to military operations posed by a basic system of independent review are not so weighty as to trump a citizen's core rights to challenge meaningfully the Government's case and to be heard by an impartial adjudicator.

The Courts as a Check Against the Executive Branch

In so holding, we necessarily reject the Government's assertion that separation of powers principles mandate a heavily circumscribed role for the courts in such circumstances. Indeed, the position that the courts must forgo any examination of the individual case and focus exclusively on the legality of the broader detention scheme cannot be mandated by any reasonable view of separation of powers, as this approach serves only to *condense* power into a single branch of government. We have long since made clear that a state of war is not a blank check for the President when it comes to the rights of the Nation's citizens. Whatever power the United States Constitution envisions for the Executive in its exchanges with other nations or with enemy organizations in times of conflict, it most assuredly envisions a role for all three branches when individual liberties are at stake. . . . Likewise, we have made clear that, unless Congress acts to suspend it, the Great Writ of habeas corpus allows the Judicial Branch to play a necessary role in maintaining this delicate balance of governance, serving as an important judicial check on the Executive's discretion in the realm of detentions. . . . Thus, while we do not question that our due process assessment must pay keen attention to the particular burdens faced by the Executive in the context of military action, it would turn our system of checks and balances on its head to suggest that a citizen could not make his way to court with a challenge to the factual basis for his detention by his government simply because the Executive opposes making available such a challenge. Absent suspension of the writ by Congress, a citizen detained as an enemy combatant is entitled to this process.

Because we conclude that due process demands some system for a citizen detainee to refute his classification, the [Government's] proposed "some evidence" standard is inade-

quate. Any process in which the Executive's factual assertions go wholly unchallenged or are simply presumed correct
without any opportunity for the alleged combatant to demonstrate otherwise falls constitutionally short. As the Government itself has recognized, we have utilized the "some
evidence" standard in the past as a standard of review, not
as a standard of proof. That is, it primarily has been employed by courts in examining an administrative record developed after an adversarial proceeding—one with process at
least of the sort that we today hold is constitutionally mandated in the citizen enemy-combatant setting. This standard
therefore is ill suited to the situation in which a habeas petitioner has received no prior proceedings before any tribunal
and had no prior opportunity to rebut the Executive's factual
assertions before a neutral decisionmaker.

Hamdi Received No Process

Today we are faced only with such a case. Aside from un-
specified "screening" processes and military interrogations
in which the Government suggests Hamdi could have con-
tested his classification, Hamdi has received no process. An
interrogation by one's captor, however effective an intelligence-
gathering tool, hardly constitutes a constitutionally adequate factfinding before a neutral decisionmaker. . . . That
even purportedly fair adjudicators "are disqualified by their
interest in the controversy to be decided is, of course, the
general rule." *Tumey* v. *Ohio*, (1927). Plainly, the "process"
Hamdi has received is not that to which he is entitled under
the Due Process Clause.

There remains the possibility that the standards we have
articulated could be met by an appropriately authorized and
properly constituted military tribunal. Indeed, it is notable that
military regulations already provide for such process in related instances, dictating that tribunals be made available to
determine the status of enemy detainees who assert prisoner-
of-war status under the Geneva Convention. In the absence
of such process, however, a court that receives a petition for
a writ of habeas corpus from an alleged enemy combatant
must itself ensure that the minimum requirements of due

process are achieved. Both courts below recognized as much, focusing their energies on the question of whether Hamdi was due an opportunity to rebut the Government's case against him. The Government, too, proceeded on this assumption, presenting its affidavit and then seeking that it be evaluated under a deferential standard of review based on burdens that it alleged would accompany any greater process. As we have discussed, a habeas court in a case such as this may accept affidavit evidence like that contained in the Mobbs Declaration [the Government's document containing statements about Hamdi's affiliation with the Taliban] so long as it also permits the alleged combatant to present his own factual case to rebut the Government's return. We anticipate that a District Court would proceed with the caution that we have indicated is necessary in this setting, engaging in a factfinding process that is both prudent and incremental. We have no reason to doubt that courts faced with these sensitive matters will pay proper heed both to the matters of national security that might arise in an individual case and to the constitutional limitations safeguarding essential liberties that remain vibrant even in times of security concerns.

Ensuring Due Process for Detained Terror Suspects

Thomas F. Powers

In the spring of 2004 images of Iraqi prisoners being brutalized by American troops flooded the media at the same time that cases regarding detained terror suspects were heading for the Supreme Court. Concern arose that the nation that values freedom above all other values may fail to afford due process protections to its prisoners and detainees.

Thomas F. Powers, a political science professor at the University of Minnesota, Duluth, has written extensively about due process and justice issues in the aftermath of the attacks of September 11, 2001. In the following selection he argues that a new policy of preventive detention is necessary in the aftermath of the Supreme Court's decisions in *Hamdi v. Rumsfeld*, *Rasul v. Bush*, and *Rumsfeld v. Padilla*. The creation of new procedures would allow the U.S. government to detain people without sufficient evidence to prove they committed a crime. However, a certain amount of due process would be provided to insure that people—citizens and noncitizens alike—are not held unreasonably or improperly.

A forthright policy of preventive detention is an idea whose time has come. This is the most important implication of the historic rulings issued by the Supreme Court in the enemy combatant cases of *Hamdi v. Rumsfeld*, *Rasul v. Bush*, and *Rumsfeld v. Padilla*. In *Hamdi*, five justices agreed that the president has the authority to detain terrorists, even when they are not charged under the criminal law and are not held as either POWs [prisoners of war] or war criminals under international law. But the court ruled that detainees who are United States citizens must be afforded greater due process protections than the Bush Administration has been willing to grant them. But the procedures called for by the court are themselves sketchy, and they relate only to the initial determination of a detainee's status.

The Administration, first burdened by [reports of abuse of Iraqi prisoners at] Abu Ghraib and now chastened by the Supreme Court, is reconsidering its policies. It has created an office charged with reviewing annually the detention of enemy combatants. Its proposed procedures, supplemented by more ambitious guidelines from the court, are a good start, but what's needed is a more comprehensive framework, authorized by Congress. America needs a USA Patriot Act for preventive detention. To get there responsibly, we should look to other countries, especially England and Israel, which have crafted preventive detention policies with meaningful safeguards for due process.

Preventive Detention Even Without Sufficient Guidance

Preventive detention means the holding of American citizens against their will, precisely because authorities do not have sufficient evidence to prove in a court of law that the citizens have committed a crime. Or when aliens detained outside the United States are involved, it means the holding of individuals neither as POWs nor as war criminals, the two categories of wartime detention recognized under international law. The last time the United States tried something like preventive detention was during World War II, with the notorious internment of some 120,000 innocent Japanese-American civilians. Doesn't the shame of *Korematsu* still burn?[1] How can that sort of detention be the take-home message of the recent Supreme Court rulings, which have been widely hailed as civil libertarian victories?

---

1. In *Korematsu v. United States* (1944) the Supreme Court declared the evacuation of Japanese Americans from the West Coast constitutional.

Preventive detention is understandably unsettling to Americans. The view favored by many civil libertarians—that the country could adopt a "criminal law purist" approach of adhering to the norms of criminal due process—has been put forth most prominently by Justice Antonin Scalia in his dissent in *Hamdi*. "If Hamdi is being imprisoned in violation of the Constitution (because without due process of law), then his habeas petition should be granted," Scalia wrote; "the executive may then hand him over to the criminal authorities, whose detention for the purpose of prosecution will be lawful, or else must release him."

The Italian Model

The purists can point to at least one modern liberal democratic country, Italy, that has used this approach successfully. The Italian government combated the Red Brigades and other terrorist groups while making only modest alterations to its system of criminal justice, mainly by enhancing police investigative powers and criminal penalties. Though the Red Brigades did not successfully advance revolutionary Marxism-Leninism in Italy and eventually faded into oblivion, terrorism in Italy during the 1970s and early 1980s was a serious matter, involving thousands of bombings, hundreds of civilian deaths, and the kidnapping and assassination of prominent businessmen and government officials, including former Prime Minister Aldo Moro.

Italy had no special interrogation policy for terrorists, developed no special courts or procedures to try them, and used no preventive detention system to get around safeguards of the criminal justice system. The police patiently gathered evidence of crimes in order to incapacitate those who committed them. If officials did not gather evidence sufficient for a criminal conviction, the terrorism suspects were released.

U.S. Needs Are Unique

But the Italian model cannot serve our needs. On September 11, the United States suffered roughly ten times the number of terrorism fatalities that Italy suffered over the span of the 15 years of attacks from the Red Brigades. Like terrorists in Northern Ireland, Spain, and West Germany, the Red Brigades used terror to effect political ends. These groups sometimes targeted civilians, but they did not seek to inflict mass civilian casualties in the manner of the current al Qaeda campaign.

The sheer lethality of the September 11 attacks, and the threat of similar attacks in the future, means that the United States needs a different sort of approach. A number of prominent legal scholars and government officials, ranging from the liberal constitutional expert Laurence Tribe to the conservative federal judge Michael Chertoff, have begun to give serious consideration to the idea of preventive detention. Even Justice John Paul Stevens, who supports civil libertarian positions, admitted in the *Padilla* case that "[e]xecutive detention of subversive citizens, like detention of enemy soldiers to keep them off the battlefield, may sometimes be justified to prevent persons from launching or becoming missiles of destruction."

What about international law? The point is not that the United States should defy international law. It must not. But under the Geneva Conventions terrorists do not fit into the only two categories provided, POW or war criminal. Preventive detention responsibly addresses the question of what to do with fighters who do not wear uniforms or otherwise distinguish themselves from civilians in combat.

The government's critics explain the Administration's current policy either in terms of some institutional perversity (executive overreach) or by reference to some pathological "authoritarianism." But the failure thus far to devise a comprehensive policy reflects, at least in part, a liberal democratic hesitation in the face of a practice that appears to be fundamentally illiberal. The time has come to face terrorism squarely, and to craft a legal response that reflects our constitutional principles.

Learning from Other Countries

Existing U.S. Department of Defense Policies extend some limited procedural rights to detainees. Most notable is the annual status review of every individual detained by the recently created Office for the Administrative Review of the Detention of Enemy Combatants. This, together with Justice Sandra Day O'Connor's insistence in *Hamdi* that all detainees be granted a hearing before a "neutral decisionmaker," and with the aid of legal counsel, provides a starting point.

How we proceed from there should be decided in light of the experience of other countries that have struggled to combat terrorism. If preventive detention is justified in large measure by the scope and intensity of the actual threat of terrorism, then England and Israel both surely qualify. More than 3,000 terrorism deaths are associated with the conflict in Northern Ireland, and more than 1,200 people have been killed by terrorists in Israel in the past decade alone.

Great Britain's indefinite internment policy, formalized in 1973 following the recommendations of a famous report authored by Lord Diplock on the situation in Northern Ireland, was allowed to lapse in 1980. Lord Diplock was reacting to a legally murky use of police power, one he termed "imprisonment at the arbitrary Diktat of the Executive Government." Though his reform proposal, incorporated in the 1973 Northern Ireland (Emergency Provisions) Act, made preventive detention a matter of administrative, not judicial, oversight, the new policy reasserted civilian control and included due process safeguards. No less a figure than the secretary of state for Northern Ireland made initial detention determinations. Within a period of 28 days, an administrative official would then review each case with the option to extend the detention. Those detained also had a right to be informed of their status hearing in advance, and they were granted the right to an attorney paid for by the government. After September 11, in the 2001 Anti-terrorism, Crime and Security Act, a limited version of the internment policy, applying only to non-citizens, was reintroduced in Britain.

In 1948 Israel inherited from the British an unofficial detention policy that was formally articulated in the 1979 Administrative Detention Law. Partly in response to provisions of international law, administrative detention is justified, as it is in England, only under a state of emergency—a status Israel has invoked and lived under continuously since 1948.

The minister of defense must authorize each case. Detention orders are issued for six months at a time and may be renewed at the end of that period. In Israel the civilian courts provide oversight, first by "confirming" the initial detention order and then by reviewing the status of each detainee every three months, overlapping with the review, every six months, by the minister of defense. Detainees have the right to an attorney, and the right to be present at their confirmation hearing and at all subsequent judicial proceedings.

A Parallel Legal System

The Policies of Britain and Israel each moved in the same direction: toward greater legal clarity and toward more extensive due process protections. The United States should take advantage of those countries' experiences to find ways to build due process into preventive detention. Current U.S. policy reflects a reactive and piecemeal approach. Designing a preventive detention policy means, in effect, creating a separate legal system that applies only to a small class of persons, a system running parallel to criminal law on the one hand, and to the laws governing POWs and war criminals on the other.

A comprehensive policy must specify standards and procedures in six key areas: 1) preliminary screening and determination of status; 2) a hearing at which detainees may challenge their status; 3) the right of appeal; 4) periodic reconsideration and renewal of status, or release; 5) general legal support, including notification and access to attorneys, evidence, and witnesses; and 6) clear standards of treatment for detainees. Some of this is already in place in Defense Department practices, but it needs to be pulled together, clarified, and made explicit for anyone who wants to know about the country's policy.

The decision as to whether individuals should be held in preventive detention can be made rigorous in a number of ways. The involvement of high government officials—the secretary of the navy in the new Department of Defense plan or the secretary of defense and even the president himself (who now designates enemy combatants)—would signal the seriousness of the process, and fixes accountability in a useful way.

Enemy combatants cannot be granted a "trial," since they haven't been charged with anything, but they should have the closest thing to it: a hearing at which they may challenge the government's claims and present a different account of the facts. As Justice O'Connor indicated in *Hamdi*, the appropriate body to oversee such a hearing might be within the executive branch, but it could also be within the federal judiciary. The hearing must be held, as O'Connor insisted, before a "neutral decisionmaker."

The right of appeal is critical to any preventive detention policy, especially for U.S. citizen detainees. Detaining Yaser Hamdi and Jose Padilla without charging them with any crime creates a greater, not lesser, obligation to justify their detention. Appeal could be made to another administrative body, or to the federal court system; a special court could serve a useful role here. In some cases, appeal or review of detention could be made automatic.

Basic Procedural Considerations

Whether it occurs every three months (as in Israel), every six months (as in Britain), or once a year (as in U.S. policy as it stands now), some formalized process for re-examining each individual case for status renewal (or release) is essential, especially in an open-ended effort like the current war on terror. Having primary responsibility for this policy, the executive branch could provide for the review process internally. Another option is a policy of external review by the courts, as is the case in Israel.

Several basic procedural rights accompany many of the steps in this process. The right to know both one's status and any procedure to challenge it, now mandated by *Hamdi*, seems elementary. A related practice, present in the current Department of Defense plan, is the notification of both the family and home country of any detained individual. Also basic is the right to be present during status hearings. The right to an attorney paid for by the government is already granted, in some instances, in U.S. policy (though not in the Defense Department plan, which grants instead the assistance of an officer who is not an attorney). Finally, if the rights to a hearing and to some sort of appeal are to be meaningful, access to evidence and witnesses, where practicable, must also be granted.

Under certain circumstances, some of these protections might need to be suspended in the name of security. But to ensure that such exceptions do not undermine the legitimacy of the preventive detention system, any decision to make such an exception to the agreed-upon procedural safeguards must itself be governed by clear standards and authorized by the highest officials. It might also be subject to automatic judicial review. The exemption process would likely need to be carried out in secret, at least in the short run. But such a procedure should go as far as possible to provide safeguards against abuses of authority for those detained.

Finally, the standards of treatment of those held in preventive detention should be laid out in detail. Rules about the limits of interrogation must be made clear to American soldiers and civilian contract workers. Similarly, how to treat prisoners held under the non-POW status should be detailed, with reference to which provisions of the Geneva Conventions do and do not apply. Israel, for example, grants better living conditions and greater privileges to administrative detainees then it does to criminal prisoners, since the former are held under a preventive, and not a punitive, regime.

Congress Should Act Now

The most important available check is Congressional involvement, through legislation and oversight. The imprimatur of Congress is all the more important now that four of the nine justices of the Supreme Court have stated, in *Hamdi*, that the current enemy combatant policy is essentially unconstitutional. Congress's silence to date on the issue has been deafening. With the exception of an effort by a handful of Democrats in the House, led by Adam Schiff of California and Barney Frank of Massachusetts, to introduce a Detention of Enemy Combatants Act, Congress seems to be happy to allow the executive branch to struggle with the problem. Congress needs to do its job, and it should write a detailed law, one to be reauthorized every five years or so.

But there's no getting around that this is a troubling area of policy. In England and Israel, preventive detention has been highly controversial. Though Lord Diplock was essentially a reformer, and though his report on Northern Ireland brought legal clarity and constraint to what he and others perceived to be runaway executive power, his name is often associated with authoritarian excess. Fashioning a preventive detention policy is likely to be a thankless task here as well. The name of the architect of America's preventive detention policy may well become associated with an innovation that will be loved by none and hated by many. But the benefit would be to bring the rule of law to bear even here, where the Bush Administration has made clear that it is only so willing to check its own power.

Even a Tyrant Is Entitled to Due Process

Robert Scheer

America's attempts to defeat the suspected September 11, 2001, terrorists and those who aided them has led to wars in Afghanistan and Iraq and to the controversial military occupation of Iraq. In December 2003, as part of this military effort, U.S. soldiers captured Iraqi dictator Saddam Hussein at a farmhouse hideout in Iraq. On June 28, 2004, political control in Iraq, as well as custody of Saddam Hussein, was transferred from the United States to the new Iraqi government. The new Iraqi justice system prepared to prosecute Saddam for various crimes, most of which were perpetrated against Iraqi citizens.

In the following selection, Robert Scheer describes the charges against the Iraqi dictator and the legal processes in place to prosecute him. Scheer describes the situation as a "travesty." He asserts that the United States, not the Iraqi government, is the de facto power behind the whole process. He believes treatment of Saddam has fallen far short of the international standards of due process that the United States, Great Britain, France, and Russia applied to Nazi war criminals who were tried for crimes against humanity in Nuremberg, Germany, in 1945.

Robert Scheer has been a journalist for more than thirty years and has taught media-related courses at several California colleges. He writes for the *Los Angeles Times* and the *Nation* magazine and is a coauthor of the book *The Five Biggest Lies Bush Told Us About Iraq*.

Has anyone noticed that the charges leveled last week [in late June 2004] against Saddam Hussein bore no relation to the reasons offered by President Bush for his preemptive invasion of Iraq? Not a word about Hussein being linked to terrorist attacks on the United States or having weapons of mass destruction that posed an imminent threat to our nation's security.

That is because after seven months of interrogation, the United States appears to have learned nothing from Hussein or any other source in the world that supports the President's decision to go to war. Washington turned Hussein over to the Iraqis without charging its infamous prisoner of war with any of these crimes. And even the Iraqis did not charge him with being behind the insurgency that almost daily claims American lives.

It's a travesty, if you think about it. The fact is that the United States, which holds itself up as the exemplar of democracy for the entire Middle East, held Hussein in captivity for seven months, virtually incommunicado, without access to lawyers of his choosing and without charging him with a crime or releasing him at the end of the occupation, as required by the Geneva Convention. If the United States believes, as most of the world does, that Hussein committed crimes against humanity, then he is entitled to the same international standards of due process that the United States and its allies applied to top Nazi war criminals at Nuremberg. It is well established in such cases that justice will not be served by turning Hussein over to be tried by his former political rivals or his victims.

America's Role in Hussein's Trial

No one will be fooled by the claim that we are merely acceding to the demands of the new Iraqi government, since its leader, interim Prime Minister Iyad Allawi, has long been on the CIA payroll and was essentially appointed to his post by the United States.

Similarly, Salem Chalabi, nephew of Pentagon protégé and discredited Iraqi National Congress leader Ahmad Chalabi, was put in charge of the trial by the United States, creating what looks so far like nothing more than a show trial.[1] The younger Chalabi is also a member of the INC, the exile organization bankrolled by US taxpayers that provided much of the now disproven "intelligence" Bush used in speech after speech to convince Americans of the urgency of the Iraqi weapons-of-mass-destruction and terrorism "threat."

Salem Chalabi was picked by Bush's national security advisor, Condoleezza Rice. In a secret directive issued in January and leaked to the public in March, Rice authorized a delegation of fifty lawyers, prosecutors and investigators to be sent to Iraq to prepare for Hussein's trial. Chalabi is not only the prosecutor but chose the judge, whose identity is a secret.

It is thus a huge stretch to call the proceedings a fair trial or an Iraqi-run affair. Men long on the US payroll are running the country and the trial; US troops are still guarding Hussein. And the United States even chose what images could be broadcast and told pool reporters they could not record Hussein's voice. An unauthorized audiotape was, however, leaked to the media.

The Nuremberg Principle

We have already grossly violated the standard of Nuremberg laid down by US Supreme Court Justice Robert H. Jackson: "That four great nations, flushed with victory and stung with injury, stay the hand of vengeance and voluntarily submit their captive enemies to the judgment of the law is one of the most significant tributes that power has ever paid to reason." But the four great nations Jackson was referring to, led by our own, were not guilty of committing aggression but rather of stopping it. The first principle of the Nuremberg trials was to hold nations accountable for crimes against peace.

It is therefore fitting that the preliminary indictment holds Hussein responsible for his aggression against Kuwait, which precipitated the 1991 Gulf War. How disturbing that in the current war it was the United States that committed aggression by invading Iraq based on false premises, thereby violating the Nuremberg principle.

1. Chalabi was removed from his post as overseer of the trial in September 2004.

The Origins of the American Bill of Rights

The U.S. Constitution as it was originally created and submitted to the colonies for ratification in 1787 did not include what we now call the Bill of Rights. This omission was the cause of much controversy as Americans debated whether to accept the new Constitution and the new federal government it created. One of the main concerns voiced by opponents of the document was that it lacked a detailed listing of guarantees of certain fundamental individual rights. These critics did not succeed in preventing the Constitution's ratification, but were in large part responsible for the existence of the Bill of Rights.

In 1787 the United States consisted of thirteen former British colonies that had been loosely bound since 1781 by the Articles of Confederation. Since declaring their independence from Great Britain in 1776, the former colonies had established their own colonial governments and constitutions, eight of which had bills of rights written into them. One of the most influential was Virginia's Declaration of Rights. Drafted largely by planter and legislator George Mason in 1776, the seventeen-point document combined philosophical declarations of natural rights with specific limitations on the powers of government. It served as a model for other state constitutions.

The sources for these declarations of rights included English law traditions dating back to the 1215 Magna Carta and the 1689 English Bill of Rights—two historic documents that provided specific legal guarantees of the "true, ancient, and indubitable rights and liberties of the people" of England. Other legal sources included the colonies' original charters, which declared that colonists should have the same "privileges, franchises, and immunities" that they would if they lived in England. The ideas concerning natural rights developed by John Locke and other English philosophers were also influential. Some of these concepts of rights had been cited in the Declaration of Independence to justify the American Revolution.

Unlike the state constitutions, the Articles of Confederation, which served as the national constitution from 1781 to 1788, lacked a bill of rights. Because the national government under the Articles of Confederation had little authority by design, most people believed it posed little threat to civil liberties, rendering a bill of rights unnecessary. However, many influential leaders criticized the very weakness of the national government for creating its own problems; it did not create an effective system for conducting a coherent foreign policy, settling disputes between states, printing money, and coping with internal unrest.

It was against this backdrop that American political leaders convened in Philadelphia in May 1787 with the stated intent to amend the Articles of Confederation. Four months later the Philadelphia Convention, going beyond its original mandate, created a whole new Constitution with a stronger national government. But while the new Constitution included a few provisions protecting certain civil liberties, it did not include any language similar to Virginia's Declaration of Rights. Mason, one of the delegates in Philadelphia, refused to sign the document. He listed his objections in an essay that began:

> There is no Declaration of Rights, and the Laws of the general government being paramount to the laws and constitution of the several States, the Declaration of Rights in the separate States are no security.

Mason's essay was one of hundreds of pamphlets and other writings produced as the colonists debated whether to ratify the new Constitution (nine of the thirteen colonies had to officially ratify the Constitution for it to go into effect). The supporters of the newly drafted Constitution became known as Federalists, while the loosely organized group of opponents were called Antifederalists. Antifederalists opposed the new Constitution for several reasons. They believed the presidency would create a monarchy, Congress would not be truly representative of the people, and state governments would be endangered. However, the argument that proved most effective was that the new document lacked a bill of rights and thereby threatened Americans with the loss of cherished individual liberties. Federalists realized that to gain the support of key states such as New York and Virginia, they needed to pledge to offer amendments to the Constitution that would be added immediately after its ratification. Indeed, it was not until this promise was made that the requisite number of colonies ratified the document. Massachusetts, Virginia, South Carolina, New Hampshire, and New York all included amendment recommendations as part of their decisions to ratify.

One of the leading Federalists, James Madison of Virginia, who was elected to the first Congress to convene under the new Constitution, took the lead in drafting the promised amendments. Under the process provided for in the Constitution, amendments needed to be passed by both the Senate and House of Representatives and then ratified by three-fourths of the states. Madison sifted through the suggestions provided by the states and drew upon the Virginia Declaration of Rights and other state documents in composing twelve amendments, which he introduced to Congress in September 1789. "If they are incorporated into the constitution," he argued in a speech introducing his proposed amendments,

> Independent tribunals of justice will consider themselves in a peculiar manner the guardians of those rights; they will be an impenetrable bulwark against every assumption of power in the legislative or executive; they will be naturally led to resist every encroachment upon rights expressly stipulated for in the constitution by the declaration of rights.

After debate and some changes to Madison's original proposals, Congress approved the twelve amendments and sent them to the states for ratification. Two amendments were not ratified; the remaining ten became known as the Bill of Rights. Their ratification by the states was completed on December 15, 1791.

Supreme Court Cases Involving
the Right to Due Process

1833

Barron v. Baltimore
The Supreme Court declares that the Fifth Amendment's due process clause applies only to the federal government, not state governments.

1855

Murray's Lessee v. Hoboken Land & Improvement Co.
The Court develops a two-pronged test to help define the meaning of the Fifth Amendment's due process clause. A procedure is considered constitutional if it is not in conflict with the Constitution and is consistent with procedures used under English common law.

1884

Hurtado v. California
The Court reduces the *Murray's Lessee* two-pronged test to a single standard. A legal proceeding is considered to be due process if the proceeding protects liberty and justice.

1897

Allgeyer v. Louisiana
The Court examines the substance of a state law regarding a restriction on entering into insurance contracts. This case is one of the first to establish a link between the Fourteenth Amendment's due process clause and the liberty of contract. Interpreting the due process clause to define a particular right that does not otherwise appear in the Constitution becomes known as the theory of "substantive due process."

1905

Lochner v. New York
The Court cites a substantive due process right under the Fourteenth Amendment to strike down a state labor law in order to protect the liberty of contract, despite the fact that the law is alleged to protect public health.

1927

Buck v. Bell
The Court finds that a Virginia law provides adequate due process, including a hearing and extensive observation, to allow sterilization of an inmate in a mental health institution.

1934

Nebbia v. New York
The Court upholds the state regulation of milk prices because the regulation is linked to protection of the public health, thus signaling an end to the *Lochner* era.

1937

Palko v. Connecticut
The Court refuses to find that the Fourteenth Amendment applies the entire Bill of Rights to state government actions. Instead, the Court asks whether the state action in question (in this case, a second trial) violates "fundamental principles of liberty and justice which lie at the base of all our civil and political institutions." The Court says that protection from double jeopardy is not such a fundamental right, and a second trial is permitted.

1938

U.S. v. Carolene Products
The Court promises to uphold economics-related state legislation if there is a reasonable inference that the facts support the legislature's judgment.

1942

Skinner v. Oklahoma
The Court invalidates a state statute that calls for the sterilization of certain repeat felons.

1947

Adamson v. California
Justice Hugo Black's dissent makes an argument for "total incorporation"—the theory that, under the Fourteenth Amendment, state governments, not just the federal government, are prohibited from violating all of the rights set forth in the Bill of Rights.

1954

Bolling v. Sharpe
The Court finds that due process prohibits racial segregation in public schools.

1961

Mapp v. Ohio
Through "selective incorporation," the Court begins to apply the protections of the Bill of Rights to the states, one right at a time. In this case, the exclusionary rule is found to prohibit the use of improperly obtained evidence against a defendant.

1963

Gideon v. Wainwright
The Court finds that the right to counsel is guaranteed even to a defendant who cannot afford to pay for an attorney.

1965

Griswold v. Connecticut
The Court states that a married couple's decision regarding the purchase and use of contraceptives is a private matter that is beyond the proper reach of the government.

1966

Miranda v. Arizona
In a group of similar cases, the Court states that evidence obtained in violation of the privilege against self-incrimination must be excluded. Any convictions based on such improperly obtained evidence must be reversed.

1967

In re Gault
The Court finds that juveniles are entitled to the same due process protections as adults.

1970

Goldberg v. Kelly
The Court finds that "property" for purposes of due process protections may include benefits from the state or other institutions, but only if the relationship creates a legal entitlement. Thus, a tenured employee is entitled to a hearing upon being fired, but a probationary employee is not.

1972

Eisenstadt v. Baird
The *Griswold* privacy right is extended to all individuals, regardless of marital status.

1973

Frontiero v. Richardson
The Court hears a gender discrimination case and states that "dissimilar treatment for men and women who are similarly situated" violates the due process clause of the Fifth Amendment.

Roe v. Wade
In the case that legalized abortion, the Court finds that a right to privacy is protected by the Fourteenth Amendment—even though the right is only implied and not directly mentioned in the Constitution.

1976

Mathews v. Eldridge
The Court formulates a test for analyzing how much process
is due in a case where competing government and personal
interests are at stake.

1980

Harris v. McRae
The Court upholds limitations on federal funding of abortions, which is interpreted by some people to limit the scope
of *Roe v. Wade.*

1986

Bowers v. Hardwick
The Court finds there is no right to privacy in the context of
a consensual homosexual relationship.

1989

DeShaney v. Winnebago County Department of Social Services
The Court finds that states are not accountable for a government program's failure to intervene to stop domestic violence
among family members.

Webster v. Reproductive Health Services
A plurality opinion authored by Chief Justice William Rehn-
quist indicates that the Court is prepared to revisit *Roe v.
Wade* in the context of the appropriate case.

1990

Cruzan v. Missouri Department of Health
The Court finds that individuals have a right to refuse medical treatment, including life support (being kept alive by artificial means), under the due process clause. However, if a
person is comatose, the Court requires clear and convincing
evidence of the comatose person's desire to terminate life
support.

James v. Illinois
The Court examines the boundaries of the exclusionary rule
and finds that illegally obtained evidence can be used to im-
peach a defendant's testimony, but not the testimony of other
defense witnesses.

1997

Washington v. Glucksberg
The Court finds a right to refuse medical treatment, but not
a right to assisted suicide.

2003

Lawrence v. Texas
The Court overturns *Bowers* and finds a right to privacy in
the context of a consensual homosexual relationship.

2004

Hamdi v. Rumsfeld
A plurality of the Court finds that people detained as "enemy
combatants" have the due process right to contest their detention before a "neutral decisionmaker."

Books

Robert H. Bork, *The Tempting of America: The Political Seduction of the Law*. New York: Touchstone, 1991.

Benjamin N. Cardozo, *The Nature of the Judicial Process: The Storrs Lectures Delivered at Yale University*. New Haven, CT: Yale University Press, 1921.

Archibald Cox, *The Court and the Constitution*. Boston: Houghton Mifflin, 1987.

John Hart Ely, *Democracy and Distrust: A Theory of Judicial Review*. Cambridge, MA: Harvard University Press, 1980.

Barbara Silberdick Feinberg, *Constitutional Amendments*. New York: Twenty-First Century, 1996.

D.J. Galligan, *Due Process and Fair Procedures: A Study of Administrative Procedures*. Oxford, UK: Oxford University Press, 1997.

Susan Dudley Gold, *In re Gault (1967): Juvenile Justice*. New York: Twenty-First Century, 1995.

Edward Keynes, *Liberty, Property and Privacy: Toward a Jurisprudence of Substantive Due Process*. University Park: Pennsylvania State University Press, 1996.

Anthony Lewis, *Gideon's Trumpet*. New York: Vintage, 1964.

John V. Orth, *Due Process of Law: A Brief History*. Lawrence: University Press of Kansas, 2003.

Lucas A. Powe Jr., *The Warren Court and American Politics*. Cambridge, MA: Belknap, 2000.

Jamin B. Raskin, *We the Students: Supreme Court Decisions for and About Students*. Washington, DC: CQ Press, 2003.

Kent Roach, *Due Process and Victims' Rights: The New Law and Politics of Criminal Justice*. Toronto: University of Toronto Press, 1999.

Sarah Weddington, *A Question of Choice*. New York: Penguin, 1993.

Howard Zinn, *Declarations of Independence*. New York: HarperCollins, 1990.

——, *The Zinn Reader: Writings on Disobedience and Democracy*. New York: Seven Stories, 1997.

Web Sites

FindLaw, www.findlaw.com. The site provides a search engine to assist with finding lawyers, court opinions, legal analysis, and other law-related materials.

The OYEZ Project: U.S. Supreme Court Multimedia, www. oyez.org. The project provides information about Supreme Court justices and summaries of important Supreme Court cases.

Supreme Court of the United States, www.supremecourtus. gov. The Court Web site provides information about the Supreme Court, cases on the current docket, and prior opinions.